Foundations in Music Theory

THE WADSWORTH MUSIC SERIES

MUSIC LITERATURE

English Folk Song, Fourth Edition by Cecil J. Sharp
The Musical Experience, Second Edition by John Gillespie
The Musical Experience Record Album by John Gillespie
Scored for the Understanding of Music — Supplemented Edition by Charles R. Hoffer and Marjorie Latham Hoffer
Scored for the Understanding of Music Record Album by Charles R. Hoffer
Talking about Symphonies by Antony Hopkins
The Search for Musical Understanding by Robert W. Buggert and Charles B. Fowler
The Understanding of Music, Second Edition by Charles R. Hoffer
The Understanding of Music Record Album by Charles R. Hoffer
The Understanding of Music Enrichment Record Album by Charles R. Hoffer

MUSIC FOUNDATIONS

Basic Concepts in Music by Gary M. Martin
Basic Resources for Learning Music, Second Edition by Alice Snyder Knuth and William E. Knuth
Foundations in Music Theory, Second Edition with Programed Exercises by Leon Dallin
Introduction to Musical Understanding and Musicianship by Ethel G. Adams
Music Essentials by Robert Pace

MUSIC SKILLS

Advanced Music Reading by William Thomson
Basic Piano for Adults by Helene Robinson
Intermediate Piano for Adults, Volume I by Helene Robinson
Intermediate Piano for Adults, Volume II by Helene Robinson
Introduction to Ear Training by William Thomson and Richard P. DeLone
Introduction to Music Reading by William Thomson
Keyboard Harmony: A Comprehensive Approach to Musicianship by Isabel Lehmer
Keyboard Skills: Sight Reading, Transposition, Harmonization, Improvisation by Winifred K. Chastek
Master Themes for Sight Singing and Dictation by Winifred K. Chastek
Music Dictation: A Stereo-Taped Series by Robert G. Olson
Music Literature for Analysis and Study by Charles W. Walton
Steps to Singing for Voice Classes by Royal Stanton

MUSIC THEORY

Harmony and Melody, Volume I: The Diatonic Style by Elie Siegmeister
Harmony and Melody, Volume II: Modulation; Chromatic and Modern Styles by Elie Siegmeister
A Workbook for Harmony and Melody, Volume I by Elie Siegmeister
A Workbook for Harmony and Melody, Volume II by Elie Siegmeister

MUSIC EDUCATION

A Concise Introduction to Teaching Elementary School Music by William O. Hughes
Exploring Music with Children by Robert E. Nye and Vernice T. Nye
Music in the Education of Children, Third Edition by Bessie R. Swanson
Singing with Children, Second Edition by Robert E. Nye, Vernice T. Nye, Neva Aubin, and George Kyme
Teaching Music in the Secondary Schools, Second Edition by Charles R. Hoffer

Foundations in
Music Theory

Second Edition with
Programed Exercises

LEON DALLIN

California State University, Long Beach

WADSWORTH PUBLISHING COMPANY, INC.
Belmont, California

ISBN 0-534-00659-0

17 18 — 84

L. C. Cat. Card No.: 68-10130
Printed in the United States of America

Preface

The second edition of this book, with programed exercises, is designed like its predecessor to teach you to read, write, and understand the symbols of music notation. These abilities open the doors to the vast treasures of music literature, past and present. The approach is equally suited to those beginning in music and those who have learned to sing and play without training in fundamentals. The material covered in this text provides a firm foundation for more advanced studies in music and an adequate background in music theory for general students, classroom teachers, and amateur musicians.

No prior training in music is presumed. All unfamiliar terms are defined, and each new concept is immediately explained and illustrated. The topical organization of the subject matter permits flexibility in the study sequence. Work in two or more chapters can proceed at the same time, and the learning of definitions from the *Glossary-Index* — a unique feature — can be interspersed throughout the course. The concise and graphic presentation of information makes it possible to include, in addition to the usual topics, sections on music manuscript, modal scales, contemporary chord structures, and jazz chord symbols.

The *Exercises to Write* and *Exercises to Perform* at the end of each chapter accelerate the assimilation of factual information and develop proficiency in the language of music. The programed exercises, which are new in this edition, serve vital drill, review, and reinforcement functions. They help to remedy individual deficiencies and to correct errors which otherwise might result in misconceptions. Valuable classroom time is thus saved for performance exercises and discussions.

All of the exercise material is suggestive rather than exhaustive. It can be modified and adapted to various individual and class requirements. The music used to supplement the examples and exercises in the book should be drawn from the student's special field of musical activity rather than from some arbitrary source. This procedure stimulates interest and encourages the application of learning to the practical problems of music. The knowledge and skill acquired in the study of music theory should always be correlated with performance and listening activities. Each singing, playing, and dictation exercise, once started, should be continued along with new exercises until the desired level of achievement is attained. The more difficult and specialized exercises are included to challenge advanced students and classes. Complete mastery by everyone should not be expected.

In the examples and exercises, whole-note symbols written on the staff without bar lines indicate that no specific rhythm or continuity is intended. All chords are to be considered as separate and unrelated, even when they appear in a series. Consideration of chord progression, chord choice, voice leading, and nonchord tones is deferred to the study of harmony, where it seems more properly to belong. The aim of *Foundations in Music Theory* is to cover a limited but essential segment of musical knowledge thoroughly and efficiently.

Contents

Using the
Programed Exercises

When you come to a section in the book headed *Exercises to Write: Programed,* cover the page with a 4 x 6 index card, which will serve as a *masking card.* Slide the masking card down the page as you read until you encounter a blank like this:_____. Wherever such a blank appears, a response is called for. Write your response above the line. If more than one blank line is exposed above the masking card at the same time, complete all of the responses before sliding the card down to reveal the correct responses printed directly below the line.

Compare the response(s) you have written above the line with the one(s) printed below the line. When your response differs significantly from the printed one, draw a line through your incorrect response and copy the correct answer in the margin. Refer back to the explanatory material in the chapter to determine the reason for your error. In this way, you can remedy deficiencies and eliminate errors before misconceptions become established. The answers corrected in the margin mark potential trouble spots for special attention and review.

1

Rhythm
Symbols

Rhythm is the one element of music that can exist independently of other elements. The symbols of musical rhythm are notes.

Notes

Relative duration in music is indicated by symbols with varied characteristics. The longest value commonly used is a *whole note.* Shorter values are identified by appropriate fractional names. Here are some of the most common notes:

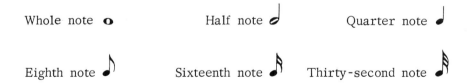

Values twice as long as a whole note or half as long as a thirty-second note are encountered too rarely to warrant detailed study.

Double whole note ⊨o⊨   Sixty-fourth note ♪

The fractional names accurately reflect the relative rhythmic values of the various note symbols. In the order illustrated, each note has a value one-half that of the previous note and double that of the following note.

1 Whole note   𝅝

equals

2 Half notes   𝅗𝅥   𝅗𝅥

or

4 Quarter notes   𝅘𝅥   𝅘𝅥   𝅘𝅥   𝅘𝅥

or

8 Eighth notes   𝅘𝅥𝅮 𝅘𝅥𝅮 𝅘𝅥𝅮 𝅘𝅥𝅮 𝅘𝅥𝅮 𝅘𝅥𝅮 𝅘𝅥𝅮 𝅘𝅥𝅮

or

16 Sixteenth notes   𝅘𝅥𝅯 𝅘𝅥𝅯 𝅘𝅥𝅯 𝅘𝅥𝅯 𝅘𝅥𝅯 𝅘𝅥𝅯 𝅘𝅥𝅯 𝅘𝅥𝅯 𝅘𝅥𝅯 𝅘𝅥𝅯 𝅘𝅥𝅯 𝅘𝅥𝅯 𝅘𝅥𝅯 𝅘𝅥𝅯 𝅘𝅥𝅯 𝅘𝅥𝅯

etc.

Dotted Notes

A dot added to a note symbol increases its rhythmic value by one-half. In other words, a note with a dot has a duration equal to that of the basic symbol plus that of the next shorter symbol.

Dotted whole note 𝅝· = 𝅝 + 𝅗𝅥   Dotted eighth note 𝅘𝅥𝅮· = 𝅘𝅥𝅮 + 𝅘𝅥𝅯

Dotted half note 𝅗𝅥· = 𝅗𝅥 + 𝅘𝅥   Dotted sixteenth note 𝅘𝅥𝅯· = 𝅘𝅥𝅯 + 𝅘𝅥𝅰

Dotted quarter note 𝅘𝅥· = 𝅘𝅥 + 𝅘𝅥𝅮   Dotted thirty-second note 𝅘𝅥𝅰· = 𝅘𝅥𝅰 + 𝅘𝅥𝅱

The rhythmic value of a dotted note is double that of the next shorter dotted note and three times that of the next shorter note without a dot, thus:

𝅝·   =   𝅗𝅥·   𝅗𝅥·   or   𝅗𝅥   𝅗𝅥   𝅗𝅥

𝅗𝅥·   =   𝅘𝅥·   𝅘𝅥·   or   𝅘𝅥   𝅘𝅥   𝅘𝅥

𝅘𝅥·   =   𝅘𝅥𝅮·   𝅘𝅥𝅮·   or   𝅘𝅥𝅮   𝅘𝅥𝅮   𝅘𝅥𝅮

Two dots added to a note increase its rhythmic value by three-fourths. The second dot adds one-half the value of the first dot to the total duration. Double dotted notes are rare.

Heads, Stems, Flags, and Beams

Heads, stems, flags and beams,* as well as dots, determine the rhythmic significance of note symbols. Heads are open ovals for the longer values and solid ovals for shorter values. Stems are attached to the heads of all notes shorter than a whole. The stems may extend either up or down from the head. The direction has no bearing on the meaning of the symbol. Ascending stems extend from the right of the head, descending stems from the left. Flags, extending to the right of stems, denote values shorter than a quarter. Eighth notes have one flag, sixteenth notes two, and thirty-second notes three.

In instrumental music it is customary to use *beams* in place of flags on groups of eighth, sixteenth, and thirty-second notes occurring within a rhythmic unit. The number of beams corresponds to the number of flags.

* *Flags* are also called *hooks; beams* are also called *ligatures.*

In vocal music, notes of these values associated with a single syllable of the text are joined with beams, as in instrumental music. Formerly, notes associated with different syllables were written separately, as shown in the next example, but current practice is to join notes in vocal music just as in instrumental music, without reference to the distribution of the text.

It came   up - on___the mid - night clear, That glo - rious song___of old.

Rests

For every note symbol there is an equivalent *rest* symbol to denote a period of silence. Theoretically the equivalent of a dotted whole note is a dotted whole rest, but in practice whole rests are used to denote full measures of silence without reference to their precise rhythmic content. For this reason a simple whole rest is given as the corollary of both the whole note and the dotted whole note. Whole and half rests are distinguished only by their position in relation to a line (of the staff). Whole rests are below the line; half rests are above. In other words, a line touches the top of whole rests, and the bottom of half rests. Dots added to rest symbols, like dots added to note symbols, increase their rhythmic value by one-half. In notating silence, the rhythmic value of a dotted rest may be (and frequently is) represented by two rests, the second taking the place of the dot, as shown in the following example.

In instrumental parts, consecutive complete measures of silence are usually indicated by a number, representing the total of such measures, centered above the symbol shown:

The Beat

The rhythmic unit to which one responds in marching or dancing—and which exists in virtually all music—is the *beat*. The note symbols commonly used to represent the beat are the following:

Other symbols for the beat are possible but rare.

In spinning the rhythmic web of music, beats are combined and divided in myriad fashion. Rhythmic values can be extended beyond a beat by any multiple or fraction of a beat. Values that cannot be represented by a single note symbol can be represented by combinations of note symbols connected by *ties*. Ties are curved lines joining notes of the same pitch. Notes connected by ties are performed as if they were a single note with a rhythmic value equal to the total of the notes thus connected.

Within a beat only a limited number of divisions is possible. Divisions are categorized as *equal* or *unequal*. Dividing and subdividing beats represented by half, quarter, and eighth notes produce the following *equal* divisions:

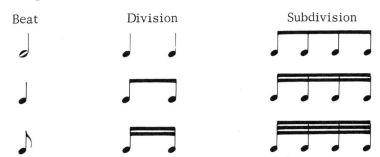

Combining various segments of subdivided quarter-note beats produces the following *unequal* divisions:

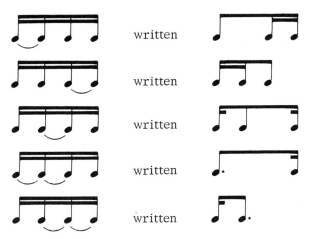

Half-note beats and eighth-note beats have the same unequal division as those shown for quarter-note beats. Identical rhythmic relationships are represented by corresponding note values—double for half-note beats and half for eighth-note beats. The unequal divisions that have the longer values at the beginning and the shorter values at the end are far more common than those that begin with the shorter values.

Beats represented by dotted notes divide into three notes of equal value and subdivide into six notes of equal value.

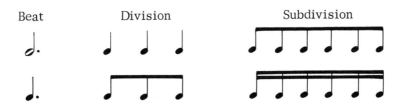

Unequal divisions of beats represented by dotted notes are made by combining pairs of notes from the equal groups of three:

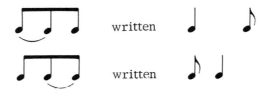

Many possibilities for unequal division are inherent in equal groups of six. The following are representative.

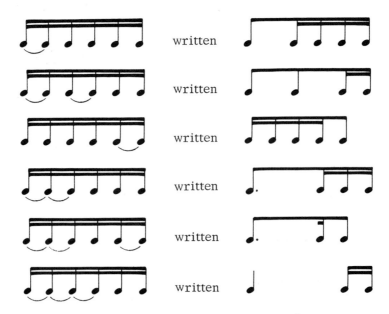

The relationships shown for the dotted quarter-note beat would prevail also if the beat were represented by a dotted half note.

Triplets and Duplets

The equal division of undotted note values into thirds is indicated by the number 3 over or under a group of three notes, as shown below. These are *triplets*.

Equal division of dotted note values into halves is indicated by the number 2 over or under a pair of notes. These are *duplets:*

Unusual and irregular groups of notes are written and named in a similar manner.

Music Manuscript

Being able to write legible music manuscript quickly and accurately is a valuable asset for everyone in music. Skill is developed by practice, but a few tips can speed the process.

The sole advantage of pencil manuscript is that it can be erased to make corrections. Ink manuscript is easier not only to read but also to write, once skill in handling a suitable pen has been acquired. The advantages of pencil and ink can be combined by doing a first draft lightly in pencil and then *inking it in* after the copy is in final form. Erasing is not necessary, but visible pencil marks can be erased without smearing the ink after it is dry.

Any fountain pen or steel nib can be used for music manuscript. Ball point pens are less suitable. Special music points are made by several companies, and certain art and drafting pens can be adapted for music copying. Music points typically make thinner lines on vertical strokes and broader lines on horizontal strokes.

Ideally, music points should spread and contract in response to slight variations in pressure to produce lines of varied width. Therefore, points designed especially for music often have three prongs instead of the usual two. A little experimentation with special pens that can be found in college book stores and in stationery, art supply, and music stores will determine which pen is best suited to your requirements. Black ink is preferred. Most India and carbon inks, which produce jet-black copy, must be flushed from fountain pens after each use to prevent clogging.

Note heads are centered on or between lines; stems are at right angles to the lines. Flags, which in printed music have a characteristic curve, can be made in manuscript as straight, diagonal lines. Beams are uniformly heavy, straight lines that parallel the general contour of the notes they connect. Properly shaped solid note heads can be made with one stroke of a suitable pen by varying the pressure as the symbol is formed, in contrast to the several strokes required to fill in the solid oval with a pencil. Open note heads are made with a single circular motion or with separate strokes for the top and bottom halves of the symbol.

Uniformity, which comes with practice, is the key to attractive music manuscript.

MANUSCRIPT PRACTICE

1. Write a line of each of the note symbols, striving to improve your music manuscript. The note heads should fill the space between the double guide lines in the manner of the models. Note heads of the same dimensions should be centered on the single guide lines. Space the notes evenly across the page the same distance apart as the models. Align the second row of each rhythmic value diectly under the first.

2. Write a line of each of the rest symbols. Position the rests in relation to the guide lines as shown.

EXERCISES TO WRITE: PROGRAMED

(See *Using the Programed Exercises,* page **x.**)

1. Name each of the note and rest symbols.

o _____ whole note	— _____ whole rest
𝅗 _____ half note	▬ _____ half rest
𝅘𝅥 _____ quarter note	𝄽 _____ quarter rest
𝅘𝅥𝅮 _____ eighth note	𝄾 _____ eighth rest
𝅘𝅥𝅯 _____ sixteenth note	𝄿 _____ sixteenth rest

2. Write the note symbol specified, and then write the equivalent rest without using a dot.

Notes   Rests

Dotted whole

Dotted half

Dotted quarter

Dotted eighth

Dotted sixteenth

3. Write one note with a value equal to the two tied notes.

4. Write a rest after the undotted notes to make the equations correct.

5. Write the rhythmic equivalent of the dotted notes, using ties.

6. Add beams to make pairs of eighth notes.

7. Add beams to make groups of four sixteenth notes.

8. Transform the quarter notes into triplet eighth notes.

9. Transform the quarter notes into duplets, each with the rhythmic value of a dotted half note.

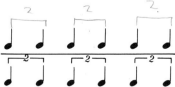

10. Write the rests equivalent to the notes and the notes equivalent to the rests.

11. Complete the table.

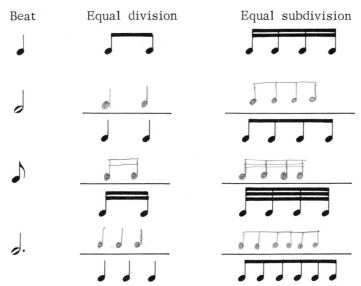

12. Give the usual notation for these rhythms substituting single notes, with dots as necessary, for the tied notes.

EXERCISES TO PERFORM

1. Establish a slow, steady beat by tapping your toe. Think of the beats as quarter notes, and clap eighth notes (equal divisions of the beat). When you become accustomed to this pattern, change to clapping sixteenth notes (equal subdivisions of the beat.)
2. Establish a steady beat as in Exercise 1. Think of the beats as dotted quarter notes, and clap three eighth notes to a beat (equal division). When this pattern is thoroughly familiar, switch to six sixteenth notes to a beat (equal subdivision).
3. Over a steady background beat clap equal divisions and subdivisions of beats alternately.
4. Over a steady background beat clap each of the unequal divisions shown in the examples on pages 5 and 6 four times in succession; then progress to the next pattern without interrupting the background beat.
5. Over a steady background beat clap duplet and triplet patterns alternately.

2

Meters, Measures, and Time Signatures

The pulses or beats of music combine into groups of varying dimensions with characteristic accentual patterns called *meters*. The end of each complete pattern and the beginning of the next is marked in music notation by a *bar line*. *Double bars*—two adjacent bar lines—are placed at the ends of compositions and major sections. The rhythmic unit between bar lines is a *measure*. The accent pattern traditionally is constant, and a *time signature* (or *meter signature*) at the beginning of a work or passage specifies the underlying rhythmic structure of the music that follows. Each metric group in music begins with an accented beat. The type of meter depends upon the number of unaccented beats and the distribution of secondary accents, if any. *Rhythm* is the inclusive term for all temporal aspects of music, including both metric groupings and duration relationships.

Simple Meters

A measure of *simple duple meter* consists of two beats, the first a primary accent, the second unaccented. The location of the accented and unaccented beats in relation to the bar lines can be shown with scansion signs.

$$\text{/ } \cup \mid \text{ / } \cup \parallel$$
$$1 \quad 2 \quad \mid \quad 1 \quad 2$$

A measure of *simple triple meter* consists of three beats, the first a primary accent, the second and third unaccented.

$$\text{/ } \cup \cup \mid \text{ / } \cup \cup \parallel$$
$$1 \quad 2 \quad 3 \quad \mid \quad 1 \quad 2 \quad 3$$

15

A measure of *simple quadruple meter* consists of four beats, the first a primary accent, the third a secondary accent; the second and fourth beats are unaccented. A dash is used to show secondary accents in this example:

$$/ \quad \cup \quad - \quad \cup \quad | \quad / \quad \cup \quad - \quad \cup \quad \|$$

$$1 \quad 2 \quad 3 \quad 4 \quad\quad 1 \quad 2 \quad 3 \quad 4$$

The beats in simple meters are represented by undotted notes which normally divide into halves.

Measures of six beats in which the first is a primary accent, the fourth a secondary accent, and the other beats are unaccented are technically in *simple sextuple meter*. More often, however, such measures are perceived as having two beats (duple) which divide into thirds. In such cases the perceived beat would be represented by a dotted note, but there is no method in conventional notation for indicating dotted-note beats. Therefore, the next shorter value is usually designated as the beat, and the beats fall regularly into groups of three. Measures consisting of two or more groups of three beats (which may be perceived as two or more beats dividing in thirds) are *compound meters*.

Compound Meters

Multiplying the number of beats in a measure of a simple meter by three gives the number of beats in a measure of the corresponding compound meter. The number of beats in a measure of simple duple meter is two. The number of beats in a measure of *compound duple meter* is six, with accents as marked:

$$/ \quad \cup \quad \cup \quad - \quad \cup \quad \cup \quad | \quad / \quad \cup \quad \cup \quad - \quad \cup \quad \cup \quad \|$$

$$1 \quad 2 \quad 3 \quad 4 \quad 5 \quad 6 \quad\quad 1 \quad 2 \quad 3 \quad 4 \quad 5 \quad 6$$

Similarly, *compound triple meter* has nine beats. The first receives the primary accent, as always; the fourth and seventh receive secondary accents, and the other beats are unaccented.

$$/ \quad \cup \quad \cup \quad - \quad \cup \quad \cup \quad - \quad \cup \quad \cup \quad \|$$

$$1 \quad 2 \quad 3 \quad 4 \quad 5 \quad 6 \quad 7 \quad 8 \quad 9$$

Compound quadruple meter, which is rare, adds another group of three beats to the pattern of compound triple meter.

$$/ \quad \cup \quad \cup \quad - \quad \cup \quad \cup \quad - \quad \cup \quad \cup \quad - \quad \cup \quad \cup \quad \|$$

$$1 \quad 2 \quad 3 \quad 4 \quad 5 \quad 6 \quad 7 \quad 8 \quad 9 \quad 10 \quad 11 \quad 12$$

Observe that secondary accents subdivide the measures of all compound meters into groups of three. Subdivision into groups of two within a measure occurs only in simple quadruple meter.

Asymmetric Meters

Asymmetric meters, such as those with five, seven, and eleven beats in a measure, are possible. Asymmetric divisions of measures with total beats divisible by two or three result from irregular spacing of the secondary accents. These possibilities, which lack uniformity and regularity, cannot be defined precisely and placed in distinct categories like the conventional rhythmic patterns. They are, however, too prevalent in contemporary music to be ignored.

Time Signatures

A *time signature,* given at the beginning of every composition and wherever changes occur, shows the meter and designates the rhythmic symbol to represent the beat. A time signature consists of two Arabic numerals superimposed on the staff in the manner of a fraction without a dividing line. The upper numeral indicates the number of beats in a measure. The lower numeral indicates the note symbol used to represent the beat. Beats commonly are represented by half, quarter, or eighth notes. These are indicated in the time signature by the numerals 2, 4, and 8, respectively. Beats represented by whole notes or sixteenth notes, indicated in the time signature by 1 or 16, are possible but rare. The upper number is always given first in naming time signatures. Thus, 2/4 is called two-four time; 3/2 is called three-two time; 6/8 is called six-eight time, etc. The table on page 18 gives the rhythmic pattern and various time signatures for all conventional and typical unconventional meters.

Simple quadruple meter with quarter-note beats can be indicated by a 4/4 time signature or by this symbol: $\mathbf{C}$. Simple duple meter with half-note beats can be indicated by a 2/2 time signature or by this symbol: $\mathbf{\mathrm{\mathbb{C}}}$. These symbols, vestiges of an older system of time signatures, have been used interchangeably with the numerical time signatures in the past, but the tendency in modern notation is to use numerical time signatures exclusively. It is customary to differentiate between the number and symbol time signatures as follows in speaking and writing.

$$\text{Four-four time} \quad \frac{4}{4} = \mathbf{C} \quad \text{Common time}$$

$$\text{Two-two time} \quad \frac{2}{2} = \mathbf{\mathbb{C}} \quad \text{Alla breve or Cut time}$$

Of the many time signatures theoretically possible, fewer than half are used with any regularity. A high percentage of all music uses one of the following six:

$$\frac{2}{4} \quad \frac{3}{4} \quad \frac{4}{4} \quad \frac{6}{8} \quad \mathbf{C} \quad \mathbf{\mathbb{C}}$$

Five other time signatures are less common but not unusual:

$$\frac{2}{2} \quad \frac{3}{2} \quad \frac{6}{4} \quad \frac{9}{8} \quad \frac{12}{8}$$

Table of Meters and Time Signatures

* It is customary to beam together rhythmic groups in compound meters when the beat is represented by eighth notes.

In a few recent publications the lower number of the conventional time signature is replaced by the note symbol representing the beat. The advantage of this new system is that it provides for the notation of dotted-note beats.

$$\frac{2}{4} = \frac{2}{\text{♩}} \qquad\qquad \frac{3}{2} = \frac{3}{\text{𝅝}}$$

$$\frac{6}{8} = \frac{6}{\text{♪}} \text{ or } \frac{2}{\text{♩.}} \qquad\qquad \frac{12}{4} = \frac{12}{\text{♩}} \text{ or } \frac{4}{\text{♩.}}$$

Conducting and Counting

Conductors use more or less standardized gestures, which vary in detail but conform in general outline, to represent the various meters. The first beat in all meters is marked by a decisive down-stroke directly in front of the conductor's body. From this point on, the patterns vary according to the meter, as shown in the diagrams on the next page.

In studying and rehearsing music, beats are often counted—in addition to or in place of conducting. The first beat of each measure is always *one,* and subsequent beats are numbered consecutively up to the total in the measure. Another method of marking the beat, though it is more practiced than praised, is tapping the toe synchronously with the beat.

When the beat is unusually slow, a more precise rhythmic interpretation sometimes is achieved by dividing the beat. In counting, division is indicated by interposing some word or syllable, usually *and,* midway between the numbers that mark the beats.

one   and   two   and   three   and   four   and

In conducting, divided beats are indicated by small motions rhythmically superimposed on the basic beat pattern. The beats of all simple meters are divided when this facilitates an accurate rendition of the rhythm. When the beat is divided, the next shorter value becomes the perceived, but not the notated, beat.

In compound meters, the notated beat is often too fast to be counted and conducted conveniently. Groups of three beats, according to the time signature, then become the perceived pulse and a suitable basis for conducting and counting. Although conventional time signatures do not indicate beats represented by dotted notes, a dotted value, in effect, becomes the beat whenever music in compound meter is too fast for the notated beats to be perceived individually as such. When this occurs, performers and listeners alike interpret groups of three beats in the notation as single beats, although no corresponding adjustment in the time signature is made. For proper understanding, however, the appropriate dotted

Meter	Time Signatures	Conductor's Beat
simple duple	$\frac{2}{2}$ (¢) $\frac{2}{4}$ $\frac{2}{8}$	
simple triple	$\frac{3}{2}$ $\frac{3}{4}$ $\frac{3}{8}$	
simple quadruple	$\frac{4}{2}$ $\frac{4}{4}$ (c) $\frac{4}{8}$	
compound duple	$\frac{6}{2}$ $\frac{6}{4}$ $\frac{6}{8}$	or like simple duple
compound triple	$\frac{9}{2}$ $\frac{9}{4}$ $\frac{9}{8}$	or like simple triple
compound quadruple	$\frac{12}{2}$ $\frac{12}{4}$ $\frac{12}{8}$	or like simple quadruple

note must be regarded as the beat. Comparing the rhythm of two songs in 6/8 time, one slow and one fast, will help clarify this point.

Drink To Me Only with Thine Eyes

Slow, beat represented by ♪

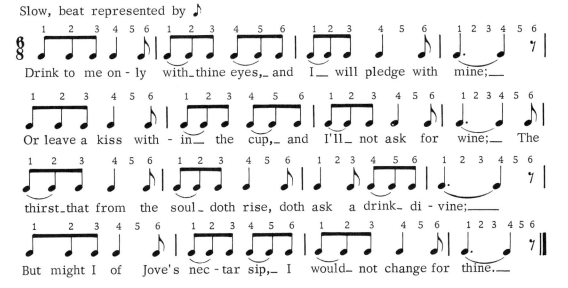

For He's a Jolly Good Fellow

Fast, beat represented by ♩.

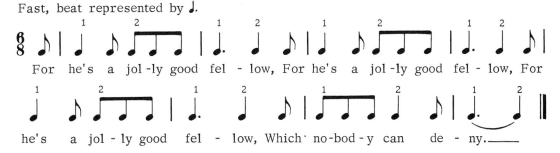

Fast 6/8 time is counted and conducted like 2/4, but the beats divide differently. Only notes that belong within beats or proper groups of beats in compliance with the time signature are joined by beams.

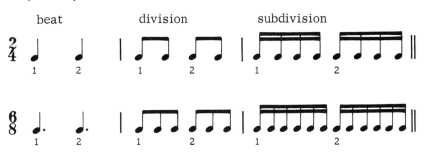

Groups of notated beats in simple meters also merge sometimes in fast tempos. The three beats in the simple triple meters are especially apt to coalesce and be played and heard as one. This produces the effect of one-beat measures with the perceived beat represented by a dotted half note.

Incomplete Measures

Within the body of a composition, measures must be complete. That is, every measure must have the rhythmic equivalent of the full value indicated by the time signature. However, it is common for the first and last measures of a composition to be incomplete. Incomplete measures occur at the beginning when one or more unaccented notes precede the first primary accent. When this happens, the first bar line is placed immediately before the first primary accent. The notes that anticipate the first primary accent, whatever their value, constitute an incomplete measure. An incomplete measure at the beginning of a piece is always balanced by an incomplete measure at the end. The two incomplete measures together equal one complete measure.

The initial notes preceding the first primary accent are termed the *upbeat* or *anacrusis.*

Syncopation

When an unaccented beat is joined to an accented beat so that the accent is not sounded, the effect is known as *syncopation.* Syncopation also results when the latter portion of a beat is joined to the initial portion of the following beat and when a rest occurs where an accent is expected. Syncopation implies a temporary lack of coincidence between the sounding rhythm and the underlying pulse, and it sometimes creates the illusion of a momentary shift in the location of the beat or the bar line. It is the hallmark of jazz and a common source of rhythmic interest and variety in the music of most styles and periods. The following examples show some typical syncopated rhythms.

EXERCISES TO WRITE: PROGRAMED

1. Give the precise designation for each of the meters.

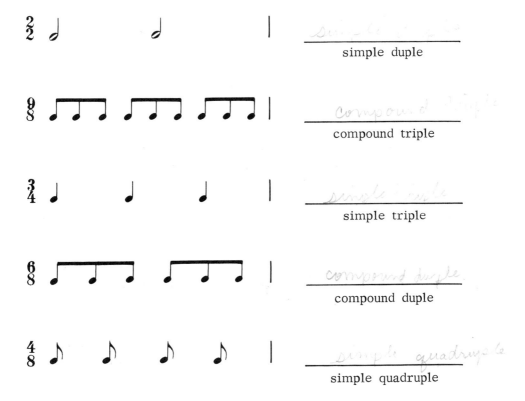

simple duple

compound triple

simple triple

compound duple

simple quadruple

2. Write numerical time signatures with the same meaning as the symbols.

3. Write appropriate note symbols to show the correct number of beats in a measure for each time signature.

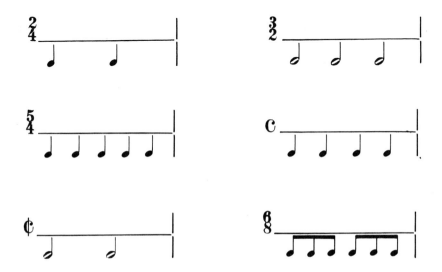

4. Show the two different accent patterns possible in the following asymmetric meter.

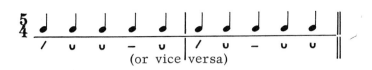

5. Show (in any order) the three different accent patterns possible in the following asymmetric meter.

6. Add bar lines, accent marks, and beat numbers in the manner of the model. When a printed bar line marks an incomplete first measure, the last measure should be a complementary incomplete measure.

7. Divide the following rhythms into measures. Draw stems up from the individual notes and substitute beams for the flags wherever possible. (Eighth notes and shorter values within a beat are always joined in instrumental music and, now, usually in vocal music as well. Notes within the same metric accent group may also be joined. In conventional notation, beams do not extend into or across metric accents, either primary or secondary.)

8. Transcribe the following rhythms substituting equivalent rests for the notes and equivalent notes for the rests. Connected and tied notes should be replaced by a single rest when possible. Individual rests, except those which occupy complete measures, should not extend into or across metric accents. Remember, whole rests are used for complete measures of silence in all meters. For additional practice after completing the exercise, replace the dots on dotted rests with equivalent rests where appropriate.

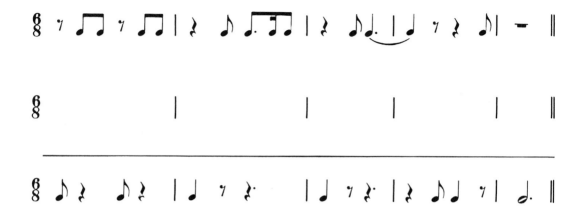

EXERCISES TO WRITE: UNPROGRAMED

1. Find a familiar song or a short composition for your performing medium written in each of the meters indicated. Using the printed analysis of *Silent Night* as a model, determine the number of different rhythm patterns used for full measures and copy each pattern once. Number the measures of the piece starting with the first complete measure and list by number the measures in which each pattern appears. (The number of different rhythm patterns in a composition is usually limited, and the repetition of characteristic patterns provides a unifying element.)

Gruber: *Silent Night*

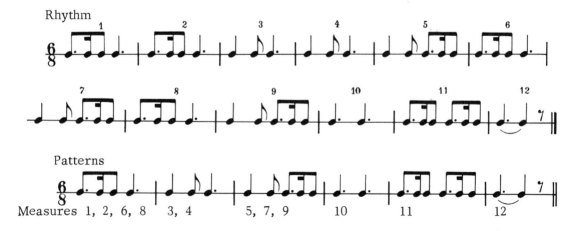

Measures 1, 2, 6, 8   3, 4   5, 7, 9   10   11   12

$\frac{3}{4}$ _____

$\frac{4}{4}$ _____

$\mathbb{C}$ _____

$\mathbb{\phi}$ _____

$\frac{6}{8}$ _____

2. Fill in the measures with notes and rests using as many different values and logical combinations as possible. Derive patterns from the previous exercise and from the recurrent patterns you detect in the music you hear and perform.

$\frac{2}{4}$ |————|————|————‖

$\frac{3}{4}$ |————|————|————‖

$\frac{4}{4}$ |————|————|————‖

$\mathbb{C}$ |————|————|————‖

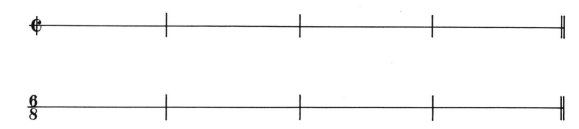

EXERCISES TO PERFORM

1. While counting aloud, tap the rhythms of all the exercises more than one measure long in this chapter.
2. Practice all of the conductor's beat patterns diagramed on page 20.
3. Perform the rhythms specified in Exercise 1 following the conductor's beat given by the teacher or a classmate.
4. While doing the appropriate conductor's beat, sing the rhythms specified in Exercise 1 with a neutral syllable such as *loo*.
5. Perform the rhythms of music related to your special interests in the manners suggested for Exercises 1, 3, and 4.
6. Distinguish between simple and compound meters and between duple and triple meters in music you hear.
7. When selected recordings are played, determine a plausible time signature for the music. Specific time signatures cannot be determined, because there is no way to tell from the sound which symbol is used to represent the beat. Also, meters such as simple duple and simple quadruple are easily confused.

3

The Notation
of Pitch

The note symbols on a page of music horizontally approximate the contour of melodic lines and vertically approximate the spacing of chords. Precise pitch meaning is conveyed by the location of the notes in relation to a *staff* with a *clef sign*. Pitches lying between those of the staff positions are indicated by *sharps* and *flats*. *Naturals* cancel sharps and flats. Sharps, flats, and naturals are known collectively as *accidentals.*

The Staff and Leger Lines

A *staff* consists of five equidistant lines enclosing four spaces. The lines and spaces are numbered independently from bottom to top. Each line and each space represents a pitch. The positions directly below the first line and directly above the fifth line also represent pitches.

Leger lines, short lines spaced like staff lines above and below the staff, are used to notate pitches beyond the range of the staff.

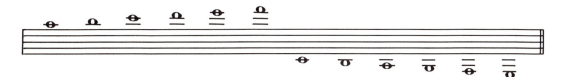

31

Stems go down from single notes on and above the middle line of the staff. Stems go up from single notes below the middle line. Stems are of uniform length except that those on notes above and below the staff extend at least to the middle line.

When two or more notes share a common stem, the direction of the stem is dictated by the note farthest from the middle line of the staff. Likewise, when two or more notes are connected by a beam, the direction of all the stems is dictated by the note of the group farthest from the middle line. The general contour of the connected notes is reflected somewhat in the slant of the beam. Other factors being equal, the preferred stemming is down.

Clefs and Letter Names

The location of notes on a staff shows relative pitch. The addition of a *clef sign* to the staff gives precise pitch meaning to each staff position. Clef signs are stylized representations of the Gothic letters G, F, and C. They show where on the staff the pitches identified by these letters are located. The G or *treble* clef indicates that the note G is on the second line.

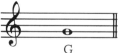

Fixing the location of the note G on the staff makes it possible to determine, through reference to it, the location of every other note. Notes are identified in ascending order by the first seven letters of the alphabet, A through G. After G the next higher pitch is A again, and the cycle is repeated.

The next note below G is F, and successive descending notes are named in reverse alphabetical order. The next lower note after A is G, and the cycle is repeated.

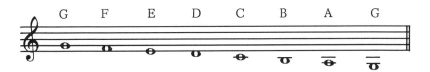

The treble clef is used for the right hand in piano music, for female voices, and for instruments such as violins, flutes, oboes, clarinets, saxophones, cornets, trumpets, and usually for French horns.

The *F* or *bass* clef indicates that the note F is on the fourth line.

From this F it is possible, as from the G in the treble clef, to determine the location of every other note.

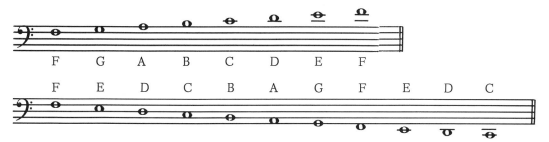

The bass clef is used for the left hand in piano music, for bass and sometimes for tenor voices, and for instruments such as cellos, string basses, bassoons, trombones, tubas, and sometimes for French horns. The harp and the organ, like the piano, use the bass and treble clefs together.

The C clef is used currently on the third line and on the fourth line. It is called the *alto* clef when it is on the third line and the *tenor* clef when it is on the fourth line. The line on which it is centered in both instances becomes the note C.

From the location of the note C in the alto and tenor clefs, the location of all the other notes can again be determined. The alto clef is used for violas. The tenor clef is used for the high pitches on cellos, trombones, and bassoons.

The C fixed by the alto and tenor clefs is midway between the G of the treble clef and the F of the bass clef. It also is near the center of the piano keyboard, so there are two reasons for its common name, *middle* C. Middle C, like every other pitch, appears in a different position on the staff with each clef sign. Its location in each of the four clefs is given for comparison in the example that follows. The relationships between the clefs are shown by a composite, with continuous lines representing common pitches.

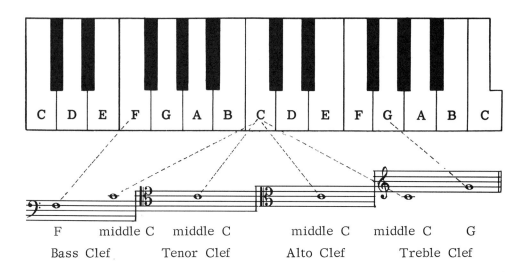

The four modern clefs—treble, alto, tenor, and bass—survived an older system in which the G, C, and F clef signs were used in various positions on the staff. In the next example, Middle C is written in each clef of the complete system.

Skill in reading the obsolete clefs is essential only for musicians dealing with old music and historical editions, but various clefs are sometimes studied and used as an aid in transposition. The treble and bass clefs predominate in modern notation, and every musician reads at least these two fluently. All musical ideas can be notated conveniently in one or the other or a combination of the two, so only the treble and bass clefs are considered further in this book.

A special adaptation of the treble clef is used in writing for tenor voices when they are not on the same staff with the basses. The written note and the actual pitch have the same letter name, but the sound is (an octave) lower. This is indicated by an "8" appended to the bottom of the treble clef sign, as shown. Formerly, a double treble clef sign or a treble clef sign with some marking on the third space was used with the same meaning, but even in the absence of such signs the special interpretation of the treble clef for tenor voices is always intended.

The Great Staff

The *great staff* consists of a staff with a treble clef and a staff with a bass clef combined. All of the most frequently used pitches can be written on the great staff or below and above it with leger lines.

A B C D E F G A B C D E F G A B C D E F G A B C D E F G A B C D E F G A

High pitches, which otherwise would require too many leger lines to be read easily, may be represented by writing a figure 8 (sometimes 8ᵛᵃ or 8ᵛᵉ) followed by a broken line over the next lower pitches with the same letter names. Pitches too low to be written without excessive leger lines are notated in the same way except that the figure 8 and the broken line are written below the notes. Where the broken line ends, the notes are again played as written. The term *loco*, meaning to play as written is occasionally added to ·eliminate any possible misinterpretation. The 8 sign is used only *above* the treble clef and *below* the bass clef.

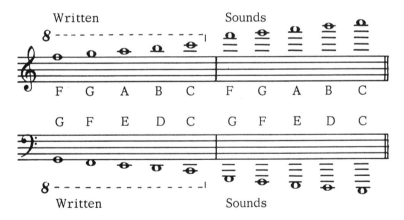

Octave Designations

Since only seven letter names are used for all the notes, obviously the same letter is used for more than one pitch. Actually, the same letter name is applied to all notes with vibrating ratios of 1:2 and multiples thereof, which sound much alike. The lowest note on a piano is A with a frequency of 27½ vibrations per second.° Notes with vibrating frequencies of 55, 110, 220, 440, 880, 1,760, and 3,520 are also designated by the letter A. The highest note on the piano is C with a frequency of 4,224 vibrations per second. Notes with vibrating frequencies of 2,112, 1,056, 528, 264, 132, 66, and 33 are also designated by the letter C. The difference in

---

° The rate at which a sound source vibrates in producing a tone determines its *frequency.* Numerical relations between frequencies are expressed as *ratios.*

pitch between any note and the next note, either higher or lower, with the same letter name is an *octave.*

There are, unfortunately, no universally accepted designations for the various octaves. Those shown in the example below are used widely. Each octave extends from C through the B above. The next higher C becomes the first note of the succeeding octave. Five-line C, the highest note on the piano, is the only note in that octave. The subcontra octave, below the lowest C, is also incomplete.

Ratio	Frequency	Letter Name	Frequency	Letter Name	Octave Designation
1	27½	AAA			subcontra
2	55	AA	33	CC	contra
4	110	A	66	C	great
8	220	a	132	c	small
16	440	a′	264	c′	one-line
32	880	a″	528	c″	two-line
64	1,760	a‴	1,056	c‴	three-line
128	3,520	a⁗	2,112	c⁗	four-line
256			4,224	c⁗′	five-line

A simpler and more logical system has been proposed and is recommended, although as yet it has not achieved wide acceptance. Starting with the lowest C, each octave is designated successively as follows:

$$C_2 \quad C_1 \quad C \quad c \quad c^1 \quad c^2 \quad c^3$$

The A and B below C_2 are A_3 and B_3. The highest C is c^4.

In ordinary parlance, musicians either call notes by their letter names without reference to specific octaves or locate them in reference to middle C, and this is sufficiently explicit for most requirements. If this were not so, communication would be more seriously handicapped by the lack of a standard terminology.

The various octaves using both designations are located on the great staff in the next example.

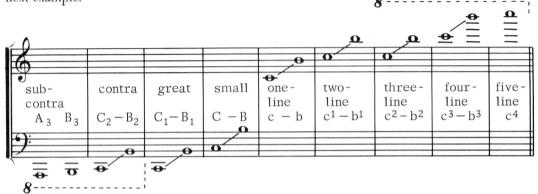

These pitches cover the complete range of the modern piano. No other instrument has a written compass so extensive, and the extremes are rarely used. Most of the pitches heard in music lie within the five central octave designations, great to four-line inclusive, or in the recommended system, between C_1 and c^3.

Sharps, Flats, and Naturals

During the period when our system of music notation was evolving, only the seven notes represented by the first seven letters of the alphabet (the ones played on the white keys of the piano) were commonly used. Five additional pitches lying between certain pairs of these seven were gradually introduced to make the same melodic patterns available at higher and lower pitch levels. These five additional pitches (played on the black keys of the piano) are recognized as inflections of the basic seven, sharing staff positions and letter names with them. In modern tuning, the twelve notes collectively divide each octave into twelve equal intervals called semitones or half steps.

Sharps and flats are used to write and name the five pitches intervening between the basic seven. A sharp (♯) is used in conjunction with a staff position or letter name to indicate the next higher semitone. A flat (♭) is used in conjunction with a staff position or letter to indicate the next lower semitone. A natural (♮) is used to cancel the effect of both sharps and flats. Sharps, flats, and naturals precede the note symbols in notation but follow the letter names in speaking or writing—C-sharp or C♯, B-flat or B♭, A-natural or A♮. All notes are presumed to be natural unless sharp or flat is specified. Sharps and flats, unless cancelled by naturals, remain in effect and apply to all notes on the same line or in the same space up to, but not beyond, the next bar line.

The twelve equal intervals of an octave are represented graphically in the next example, and the letter names, with sharps and flats as required, are given. Below each letter name the pitch is notated in the treble and bass clefs.

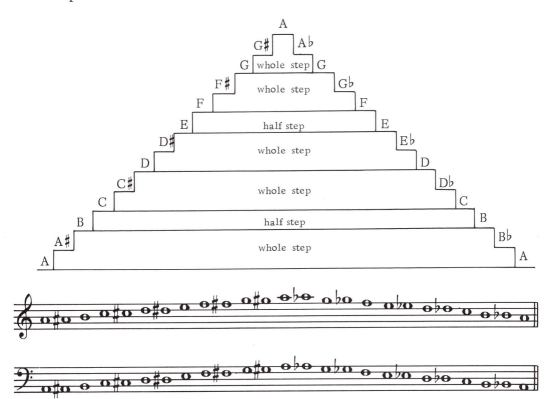

The interval between any two consecutive notes of the example is a semitone or half step. Observe that notes requiring a sharp or a flat (the black keys on the piano) separate the pairs A–B, C–D, F–G, and G–A, but that the pairs B–C and E–F are adjacent. The latter two, B–C and E–F, form the natural half steps—the only half steps between two notes both of which are naturals. The interval between the other pairs, separated by a sharp note or a flat note, is a *whole step* or a *whole tone*. The series of uninflected letter names A B C D E F G A does not represent a series of equal intervals but five whole steps and two half steps.

Enharmonic Notes

Observe in the preceding example that the A-sharp between A and B ascending is on the same pitch level as the B-flat between B and A descending. A-sharp and B-flat are two ways of representing the same pitch. *Enharmonic* is the term denoting different ways of notating and naming the same pitch. A-sharp is an enharmonic spelling of B-flat. In the same way, C-sharp is an enharmonic spelling of D-flat, F-sharp of G-flat, G-sharp of A-flat, and vice versa.

Reference to the piano keyboard helps to clarify the concept of enharmonic spelling, and its design reflects the location of the natural half steps and whole steps. On the piano keyboard the basic letter names are all on white keys, and the sharps and flats are all on black keys. The black key takes its name from the white key immediately below, raised a half step by a sharp, or from the white key immediately above, lowered a half step by a flat.

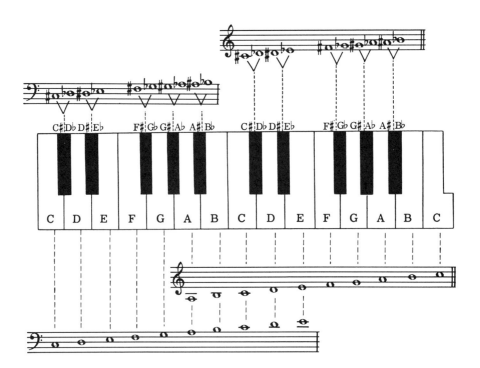

On the piano keyboard the black keys are arranged in alternate groups of two and three—a feature that facilitates locating notes on the piano.

Although there is no black key directly above B or E, each can be raised by a sharp. B-sharp is the enharmonic equivalent of C, and E-sharp is the enharmonic equivalent of F. Neither C nor F has a black key directly below, but each can be lowered by a flat, becoming the enharmonic equivalents of B and E, respectively.

Enharmonic equivalents are not completely interchangeable, for reasons that become evident when keys, scales, and chords are studied, but in practice they are regarded as the same pitch. The natural notes together with all the sharp and flat notes produce enharmonic equivalents for all the pitches except A, D, and G. Notes and letter names with the same pitch are aligned in the following example.

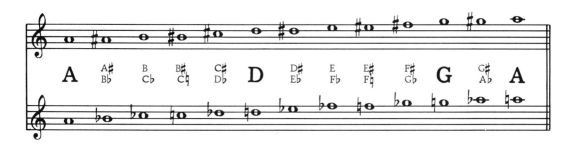

A, D, and G can be written enharmonically through the use of *double-sharps* and *double-flats*. A double-sharp (✗) raises the pitch twice as much as a sharp— that is, a whole step. A double-flat (♭♭) lowers the pitch twice as much as a flat, also a whole step. G-double-sharp and B-double-flat are enharmonic with A. C-double-sharp and E-double-flat are enharmonic with D. F-double-sharp and A-double-flat are enharmonic with G. The other pitches also have enharmonic equivalents using double-sharps and double-flats. For theoretical correctness, double-sharps and double-flats are occasionally required and do appear in musical notation. The contemporary trend is to substitute the simpler enharmonic equivalent, even though it may be technically incorrect. This practice is not recommended in writing exercises.

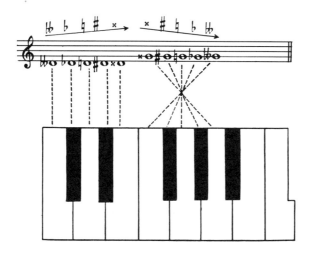

EXERCISES TO WRITE: PROGRAMED

1. Add stems properly to the note heads.

2. Add stems and beam the notes as pairs of eighth notes.

3. Add stems and beam the notes in groups of three eighths.

4. Add stems and beam the notes in groups of four sixteenths.

min.

1. prime
2. second
3. ~~Sime~~ major third
4. major third
5. fourth
6. tritone
7. fifth
8. minor sixth
9. major sixth
10. minor seventh
11. major seventh
12. eighth

Same note   prime
⊘ half-step between)   minor second
⊘ half steps between   major second

3

0 minor second
1 major second
2 minor third
3 major third
4 fourth
5 tritone
6 fifth
7 minor sixth
8 major sixth
9 minor seventh
10. major seventh

5. Write the letter names of the lines and spaces directly on both staffs as if they were notes.

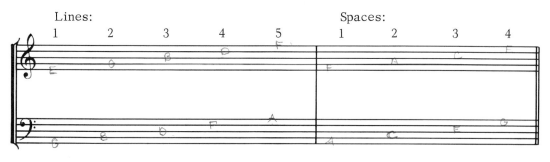

6. Write a line of treble clef signs. It is not necessary to duplicate the details of the printed symbols, but preserve the general contour, the relative size, and the position on the staff.

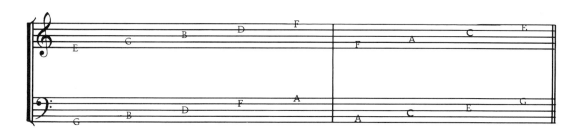

7. Write a line of bass clef signs following the suggestions given for treble clef signs. The dots on each side of the fourth line are essential features.

8. Write the letter names below the notes.

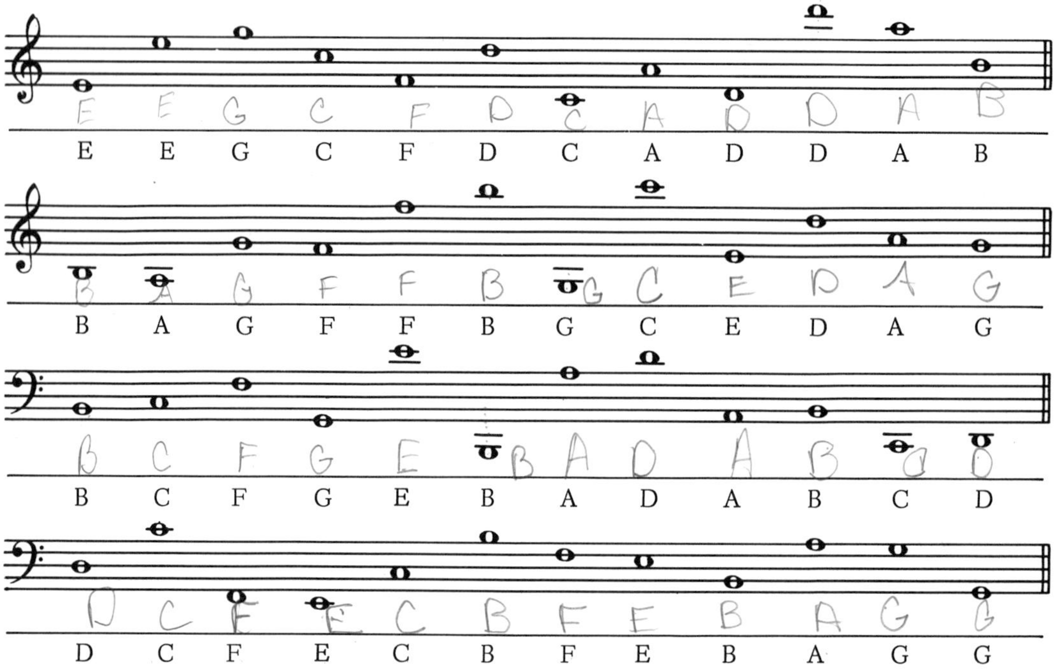
E E G C F D C A D D A B
B A G F F B G C E D A G
B C F G E B A D A B C D
D C F E C B F E B A G G

9. Add the necessary indications to make these notes sound an octave higher.

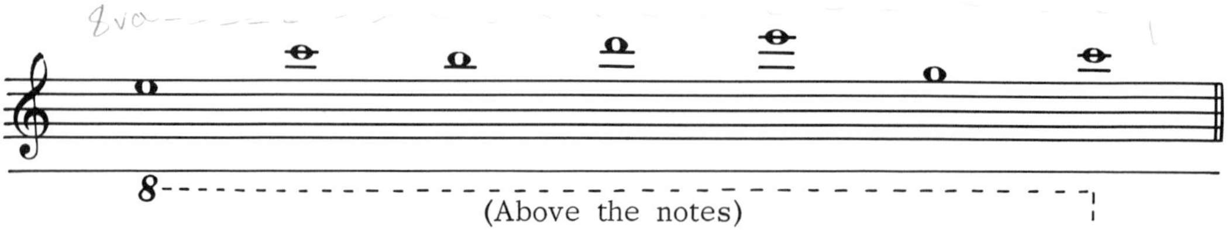
8
(Above the notes)

10. Add the necessary indications to make these notes sound an octave lower.

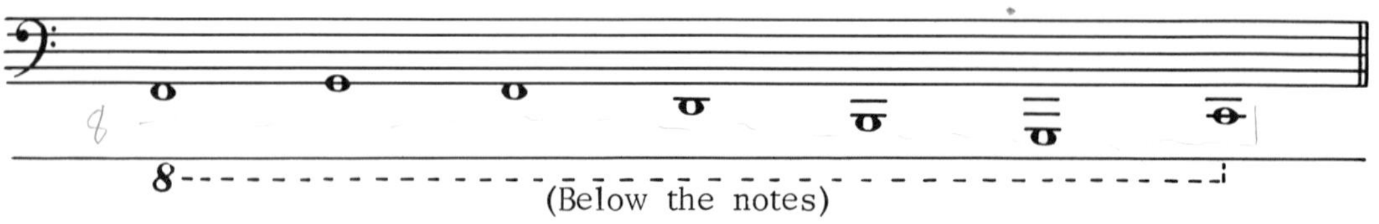
8
(Below the notes)

11. Write the notes indicated on the great staff in as many octaves as possible without using octave signs or more than two leger lines. Write the same pitches in both clefs where possible within these limitations.

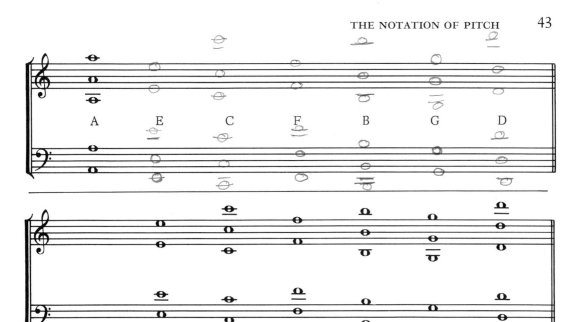

A   E   C   F   B   G   D

12. Using the system designated by the teacher or the one of your choice, give the letter name and indicate the specific octave of the notes.

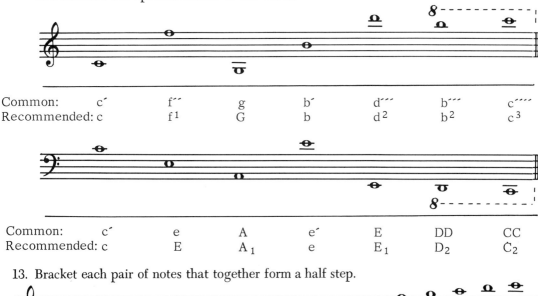

Common:	c´	f´´	g	b´	d´´´	b´´´	c´´´´
Recommended: c		f¹	G	b	d²	b²	c³

Common:	c´	e	A	e´	E	DD	CC
Recommended: c		E	A₁	e	E₁	D₂	C₂

13. Bracket each pair of notes that together form a half step.

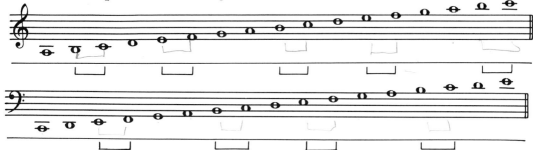

14. To each note add a sharp sign of the proper shape and size and in the proper position in relation to the note it modifies.

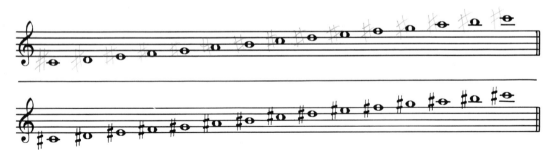

15. To each note add a flat sign of the proper shape and size and in the proper position in relation to the note it modifies.

16. Write the enharmonic equivalents of the given notes.

17. Write middle C on the staff in each clef.

18. Write the treble clef notes in the bass clef and the bass clef notes in the treble clef.

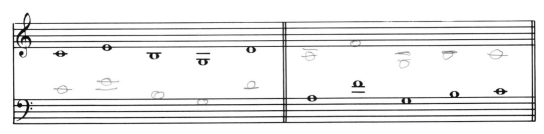

19. Add sharps as necessary to make half steps between all consecutive notes.

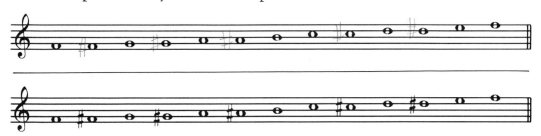

20. Add flats as necessary to make half steps between all consecutive notes.

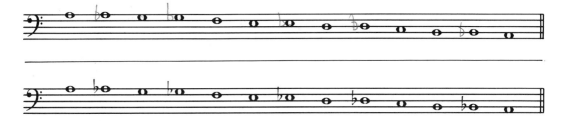

EXERCISES TO PERFORM

1. Read rhythmically with letter names some melodies written in the treble clef and some written in the bass clef.
2. Locate on the piano any note, including those with sharps and flats, when the letter name and octave are specified.
3. When notes near the center of a specific octave are played, identify the octave by sound.
4. Locate the half steps by sound when a series of consecutive white keys on the piano is played ascending or descending.
5. Play on the piano melodic lines written in the treble and bass clefs.

4

Chromatic
and Major Scales

A *scale* is a series of musical tones with fixed relationships, arranged in ascending or descending order. A specific scale establishes within an octave a pattern of intervals that is duplicated in all octaves.

The Chromatic Scale

The all-inclusive scale that utilizes in succession every pitch available in conventional notation and playable on modern instruments is the *chromatic* or *duodecuple* (meaning twelve-tone) scale. In chromatic scales the intervals between all adjacent tones are half steps, indicated in subsequent examples by the letter "H" or the mark ∧.

The example below shows the chromatic scale from C to C written with sharps ascending and flats descending to illustrate the possibilities of enharmonic spelling. The notes 2, 4, 7, 9, and 11 that are written as sharps in the ascending scale are written enharmonically as flats in the descending scale. The pattern of intervals is the same in both directions. Note 13 duplicates note 1 an octave higher, so there are only twelve different notes in a chromatic scale.

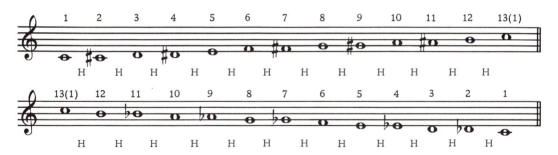

47

When scale degrees are identified by number, the numbers are taken from the ascending order. Scales ordinarily are given in ascending order only unless the pitches descending are different.

Syllable names are used in addition to letters and numbers to identify notes. Syllables in this country,* like numbers but unlike letters, are used to show location and relationship within a scale. There are seven syllable names corresponding to the seven diatonic notes —C, D, E, F, G, A, and B. The vowel sounds of the syllables are modified to show sharp and flat chromatic inflections of these notes.

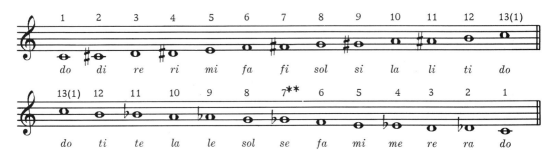

The Major Scale

Except for the chromatic scale, all the scales of conventional music are selective. That is, they use a selection of tones from the total available. Typically they are seven-tone scales with five whole steps and two half steps between their successive tones. The type of scale is determined by the location of the whole steps and half steps in relation to the starting note. Predominant among the scales of Western music is the *major* scale.

The pattern of the major scale is produced by notes 1, 3, 5, 6, 8, 10, 12, and 13 of the chromatic scale, with notes 2, 4, 7, 9, and 11 omitted. There are half steps in the pattern where successive notes of the chromatic scale are used and whole steps where alternate notes of the chromatic scale are used. Note 8 of the major scale duplicates note 1 an octave higher, so there are only seven different notes in major scales. Whole steps are indicated in subsequent examples by the letter "W."

Included in major scale

* In France and Italy similar syllables are used as we use letter names. *Do* is always C, *re* always D, etc., regardless of the scale or key. This is called the *fixed do* system. It contrasts with the *movable do* system in which the location of *do*, and consequently of all the syllables, varies with and is determined by the key. We use the *movable do* principle with syllables and the *fixed do* principle with letter names to secure the advantages of both. Our system of letter names is the same as that used in England and similar to that used in Germany.

** This note, *se*, is rarely written. The pitch traditionally is represented by the enharmonic sharp note, *fi*.

The pattern of the major scale is also produced by the notes starting from C without sharps or flats, and by the white keys of the piano starting from C. When the notes of the major scale are numbered from 1 to 8, the half steps occur between 3 and 4 and between 7 and 8, with whole steps elsewhere.

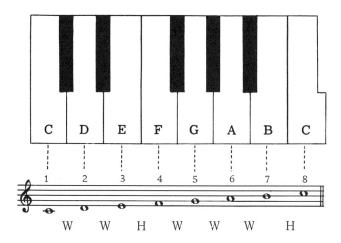

A scale is identified by type and by the note on which it begins and ends. The major scale that begins and ends on C is the C *major scale*. The note on which a scale begins and ends is called the *keynote*. Thus, C is the keynote of the C major scale.

It is useful to be thoroughly familiar with all three designations for the notes of major scales—letters names, syllable names, and numbers—because their functions are different. Letter names are constant, unchanged by the scale or their location in it. Syllable names and number designations change with the scale and show relationship within the scale and to the keynote.

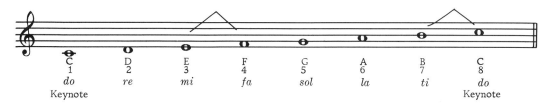

The half steps in all major scales come between 3 (*mi*) and 4 (*fa*) and between 7 (*ti*) and 8 (*do*). In the C major scale these half steps correspond with the natural half steps E–F and B–C. To produce the major scale pattern starting on notes other than C, sharps or flats are required. This can be illustrated by writing the chromatic scale starting from any note and selecting from it those pitches that form the major scale pattern.

The twelfth note of the chromatic scale starting from G is F-sharp, so the G major scale requires F-sharp. The letter names of its components are, in order: G, A, B, C, D, E, F-sharp, G. The half steps are between B and C (*mi–fa*) and F-sharp and G (*ti–do*).

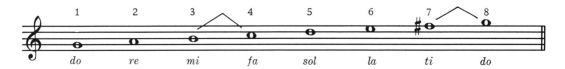

Deriving the F major scale and certain other major scales from the chromatic scale poses a slight additional problem.

The F major scale would seem to require both A and A-sharp while skipping B. However, fundamental principles underlying the construction of major and most other selective scales dictate that every letter name must be used and that none may be used more than once. To conform to these principles, the enharmonic spelling of A-sharp (B-flat) must be used. Both the reptition of A and the omission of B are thereby corrected.

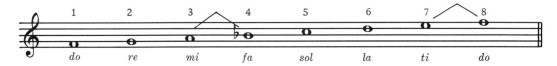

Major scales can also be constructed by adding sharps or flats as required to produce the proper pattern of whole and half steps between any consecutive series of eight notes. For example, the notes without sharps or flats between D and D have half steps between 2 and 3 and between 6 and 7.

Adding a sharp to the F produces a whole step between 2 and 3 and a half step between 3 and 4, both required for the major scale pattern. In the same way, adding a sharp to the C produces a whole step between 6 and 7 and a half step between 7 and 8, also required for the major scale pattern. Thus the notes of the D major scale are D, E, F-sharp, G, A, B, C-sharp, D.

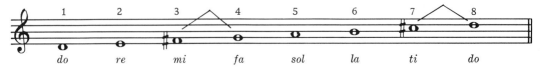

Scales beginning and ending on flat notes or sharp notes are constructed in the same way. The scale starting and ending on B-flat has half steps between 4 and 5 and between 7 and 8 if no other flats are added.

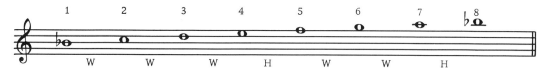

Adding a flat to the E relocates the half step to its proper position for the major scale pattern—between 3 and 4. No other alteration is required.

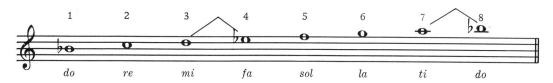

Some complete scales, like individual notes, can be written enharmonically. Observe that major scales that require sharps use only sharps and that major scales that require flats use only flats. In major scales, sharps and flats are never mixed.

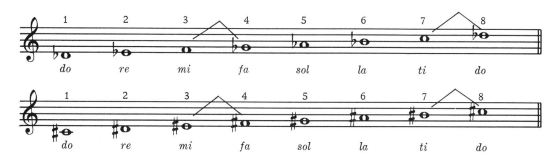

EXERCISES TO WRITE: PROGRAMED

1. Write one-octave chromatic scales, ascending with sharps and descending with flats, continuing from the given notes. Use natural notes (neither sharp nor flat) wherever possible.

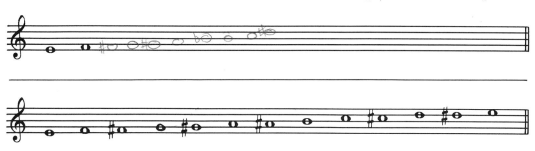

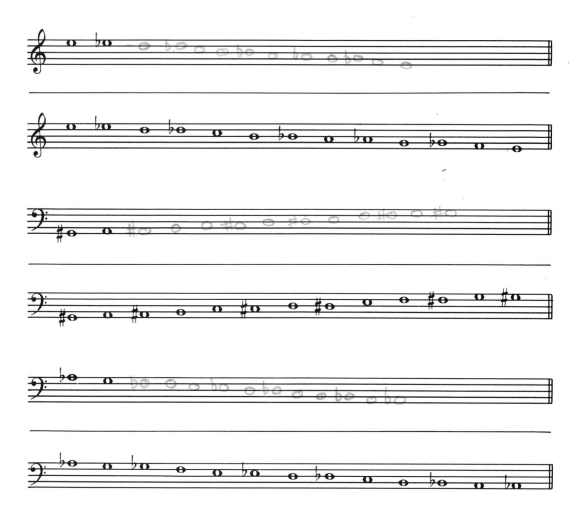

2. Mark the whole steps (W) and the half steps (H) in the following two-octave scales.

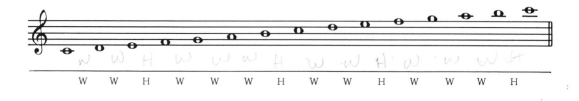

W   W   H   W   W   W   H   W   W   H   W   W   W   H

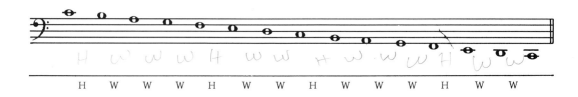

H   W   W   W   H   W   W   H   W   W   W   H   W   W

3. Write first the number names and then the syllable names under the notes of the E-flat major scale.

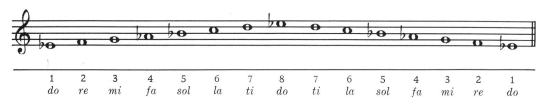

1	2	3	4	5	6	7	8	7	6	5	4	3	2	1
do	re	mi	fa	sol	la	ti	do	ti	la	sol	fa	mi	re	do

4. Write the syllable names under the notes of the chromatic scales beginning and ending on C.

do	di	re	ri	mi	fa	fi	sol	si	la	li	ti	do

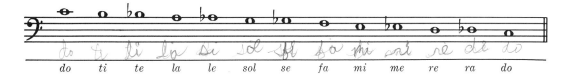

do	ti	te	la	le	sol	se	fa	mi	me	re	ra	do

5. Add sharps or flats as required to make major scale patterns in both the treble and bass clefs. Mark the half steps.

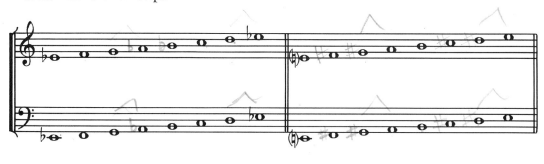

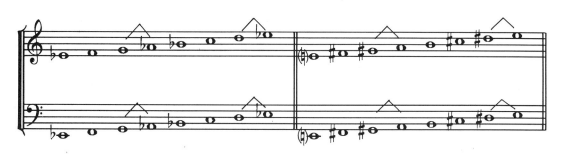

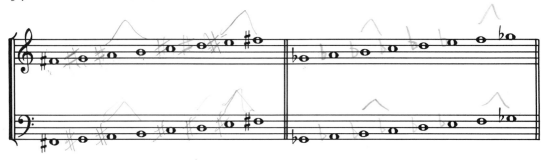

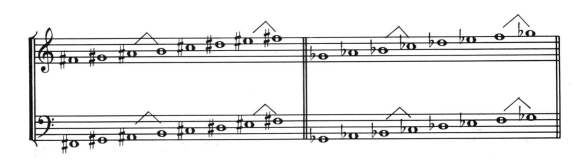

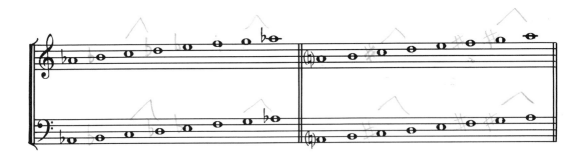

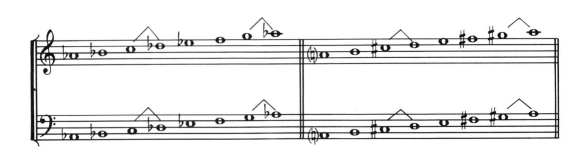

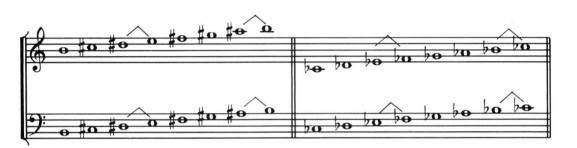

EXERCISES TO PERFORM

1. Reading from the examples in the chapter and from the programed exercises, play all of the major scales on the piano.
2. Without reference to notation, play on the piano or other instrument a major scale, ascending and descending, starting on each note of the chromatic scale in turn.
3. When a starting pitch is given, sing a major scale ascending and descending with numbers and syllables. Strive to associate each number and syllable name with its position in the scale and with its relationship to the keynote. Start the scales from various pitches throughout the vocal range.
4. Reading from the examples and from the programed exercises, sing major scales with letter names, adding "sharp" or "flat" to the letters as required.
5. When scale patterns like the following are played, indicate by number which note departs from the major scale pattern and by an arrow whether the note should be raised or lowered to conform to the major scale pattern.

Answer: 7 ↑   Answer: 4 ↓

5

Major Key
Signatures

Sharps or flats that are used consistently in a piece of music are not placed individually in front of each note requiring them. Rather, they are placed together at the beginning of each line of music as a *key signature*. Each sharp or flat in a key signature is on a specific line or in a specific space and applies to all notes of that letter name, regardless of the octave, unless cancelled by a natural. Naturals cancel the sharps or flats of the key signature only for the measure and the octave in which they appear. Natural signs are repeated when the same natural note appears in other octaves and in subsequent measures.

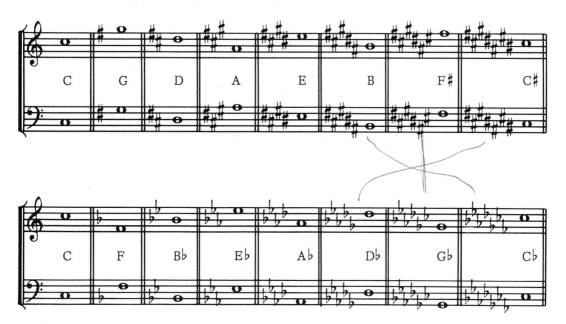

The sharps and flats of the key signature are placed on the staff in a prescribed sequence and position. Each signature is associated with one major key identified by its keynote —the note on which its scale begins and ends. All other notes of the scale gravitate to the keynote, and, since melodies usually end on the keynote, it is readily identifiable both aurally and visually. All major key signatures with their keynotes and letter names are shown in the bass and treble clefs in the preceding example.

Determining the Keynote and Signature

The keynote of a major key can be determined from the key signature. The keynote of a sharp key is always a half step above the last sharp. In other words, the last sharp in the key signature is 7 (*ti*) of the scale, and 8 (*do*) is directly above it. The keynote of a flat key is the same as the penultimate flat in the signature. The last flat in the key signature is 4 (*fa*) of the scale; to locate the keynote, go down the scale, 4-3-2-1 (*fa-mi-re-do*), or up the scale, 4-5-6-7-8 (*fa-sol-la-ti-do*), to the keynote.

To ascertain the major key signature of any keynote, write a scale up from the keynote and determine which sharps or flats are required to form the major scale pattern. Observe that all of the flat keys except F begin on flat notes. All of the natural keynotes except C and F require sharp key signatures.

The sequence of sharp major keys emerges when the notes on alternate ascending staff lines starting from the C below the bass staff are designated in turn as keynotes. When two half steps are encompassed, the next keynote is a sharp. The sequence of flat major keys emerges when the notes on alternate descending staff lines starting from the C above the treble staff are designated as keynotes. When two half steps are encompassed, the next keynote is a flat.

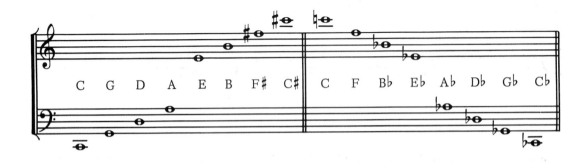

When the last three sharp keynotes are written enharmonically as flat keynotes and the series of ascending fifths (the interval between successive notes) is continued, the sequence of flat keys emerges in order from seven to none. The series then starts on C, goes by fifths through all the sharp keys and all the flat keys, and completes a circle back to C. This is called the *circle of fifths*.

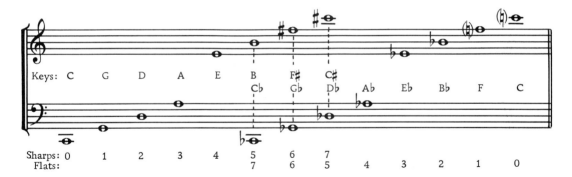

The circle of fifths is represented graphically below. Concentric circles are arranged to show all of the keys, both major and minor (which are considered in the next chapter), together with enharmonic relationships and the number of flats or sharps required by each.

Circle of Fifths

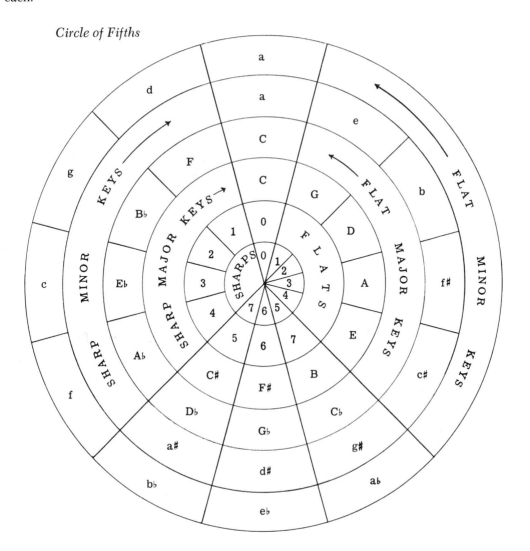

The order of the letter names of flat keys is the reverse of that of the sharp keys. The keynotes that are natural in the sharp keys are flat in the flat keys. The keynotes that are sharp in the sharp keys are natural in the flat keys. The total number of sharps and/or flats for the two major keys with the same letter name, but a half step apart, is seven.

Major key:	C	G	D	A	E	B	F♯	C♯
Sharps:	0	1	2	3	4	5	6	7

Major key:	C♭	G♭	D♭	A♭	E♭	B♭	F	C
Flats:	7	6	5	4	3	2	1	0

Tetrachords—The Sequence of Sharps and Flats

Four-note segments of scales called *tetrachords* are sometimes used in constructing scales, and they are useful in arriving at the sequence of sharps and flats in key signatures. Major scales consist of two similar tetrachords with a whole step between them. Both tetrachords of major scales have W-W-H patterns.

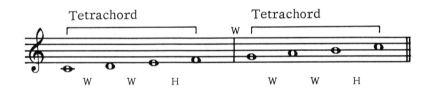

Each tetrachord with a W-W-H pattern may serve both as the lower tetrachord of one major scale and as the upper tetrachord of another major scale. The higher of two such major scales with a common tetrachord requires one more sharp than the lower scale, and the additional sharp is always required on the penultimate note of the high scale to make the tetrachord and the scale conform to the desired pattern.

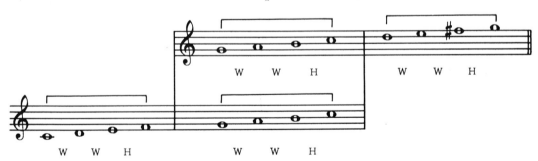

When the upper tetrachord of each major scale, starting with C, is used in turn as a lower tetrachord, the resulting series of scales introduces all seven sharps in the proper order. A note once sharped retains the sharp in all succeeding octaves.

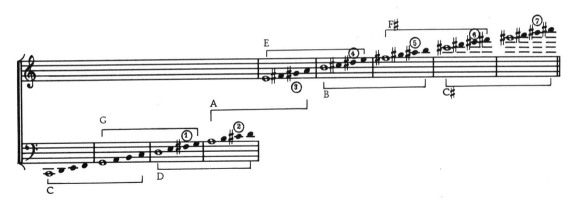

When major scales are arranged in the ascending order of the previous example, the keynotes fall, and the sharps are introduced, on alternate lines of the staff. The sharps in key signatures occur in the same order (F , C , G , D , A , E , B), but they are arranged on one staff without leger lines, as in the following example.

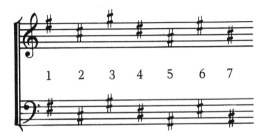

The order of whole and half steps is reversed in descending major scales and tetra-chords.

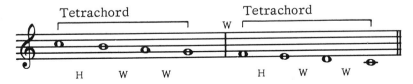

Each tetrachord with an H-W-W pattern descending may serve both as the upper tetrachord of one major scale and as the lower tetrachord of another major scale. The lower of two such descending major scales with a common tetrachord requires one more flat than the higher scale, and the additional flat is always required on the first note of the lower tetra-chord to make the tetrachord and the scale conform to the desired pattern.

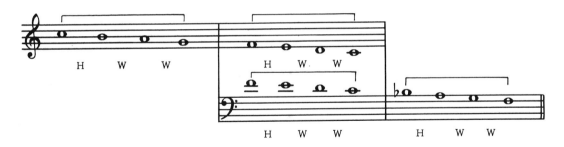

When the lower tetrachord of each descending major scale, starting with C, is used in turn as an upper tetrachord, the resulting series of scales introduces in the proper sequence all seven flats. A note once flatted retains the flat in all succeeding octaves.

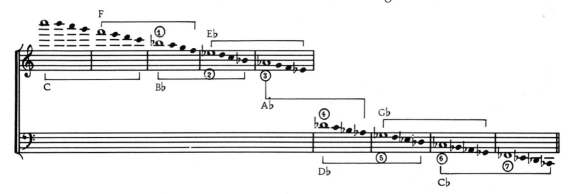

The flats, like the keynotes, fall on alternate spaces of the staff when arranged in the descending order of the previous example. The same letter names are represented in the same order in flat key signatures, but they are arranged on the staff without leger lines, as in the following pattern.

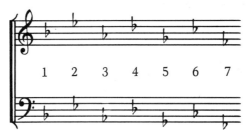

The sequence of major keys and of the sharps and flats should be memorized eventually. The following example is given as an aid to memory and as a device useful in arriving at certain factual information related to major scales and keys. The fact that alternate sharps and keynotes in sharp keys progress up by whole steps and that alternate flats and keynotes in flat keys progress down by whole steps facilitates learning, once the points of departure are thoroughly familiar.

	Sharp:		F♯		G♯		A♯		B♯
	Odd number of sharps:		1		3		5		7
	Keynote:		G		A		B		C♯
SHARP KEYS									
	Sharp:			C♯		D♯		E♯	
	Even number of sharps:	0		2		4		6	
	Keynote:	C		D		E		F♯	

	Flat:		B♭		A♭		G♭		F♭
	Odd number of flats:		1		3		5		7
	Keynote:		F		E♭		D♭		C♭
FLAT KEYS									
	Flat:			E♭		D♭		C♭	
	Even number of flats:	0		2		4		6	
	Keynote:	C		B♭		A♭		G♭	

EXERCISES TO WRITE: PROGRAMED

1. Give the letter names of the major keys with the indicated number of sharps in the key signature.

Sharps:	0	1	2	3	4	5	6	7
Key:	C	G	D	A	E	B	F#	C#

2. Give the letter names of the major keys with the indicated number of flats in the key signature.

Flats:	0	1	2	3	4	5	6	7
Key:	C	F	Bb	Eb	Ab	Db	Gb	Cb

3. Give the letter names of the sharps in the order of their appearance in major key signatures.

Order:	1	2	3	4	5	6	7
Sharp:	F#	C#	G#	D#	A#	E#	B#

4. Give the letter names of the flats in the order of their appearance in major key signatures.

Order:	1	2	3	4	5	6	7
Flat:	Bb	Eb	Ab	Db	Gb	Cb	Fb

5. Bracket the tetrachords in the ascending A major scales and mark the whole (W) and half (H) steps.

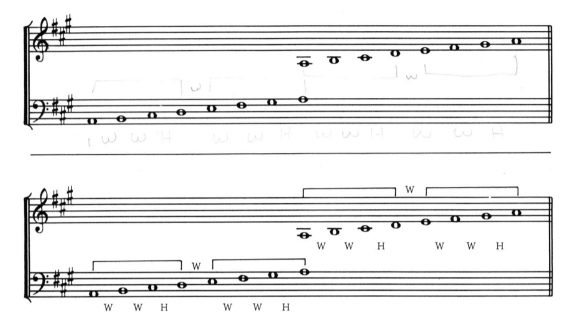

6. Bracket the tetrachords in the descending E-flat major scales and mark the whole (W) and half (H) steps.

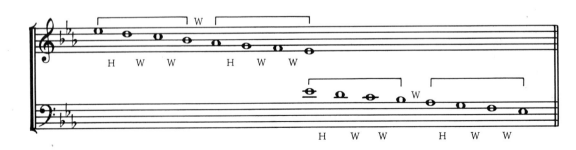

7. Name the major keys and write the keynotes on the staff for the following key signatures. If possible without using leger lines, write the keynote in two places.

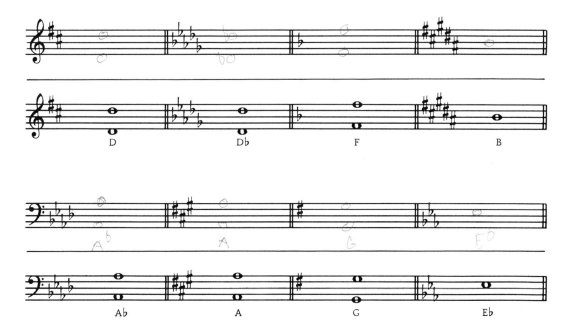

D   Db   F   B

Ab   A   G   Eb

8. Write the key signatures for the major keys with the following keynotes. After the key signatures are added, the sharps and flats on the keynotes are unnecessary but remain as part of the letter name.

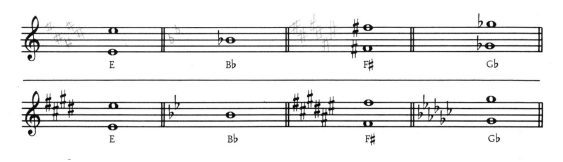

E   Bb   F♯   Gb

E   Bb   F♯   Gb

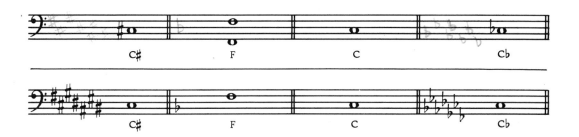

C♯   F   C   Cb

C♯   F   C   Cb

EXERCISES TO WRITE: UNPROGRAMED

1. Find a composition using each of the key signatures, or as many as possible in available music. Write the first and last note of the melody on the staff. If the melody is written in the bass clef, the first and last notes may be written one or two octaves higher in the treble clef. Name the composer or source and give the title of the composition. (Note: If the first and/or last note of the melody appears to be the sixth degree, *la,* of the major scale, the key probably is minor rather than major. Minor scales are explained in Chapter 6.)

Key signature	First note	Last note	Composer or source	Title of composition

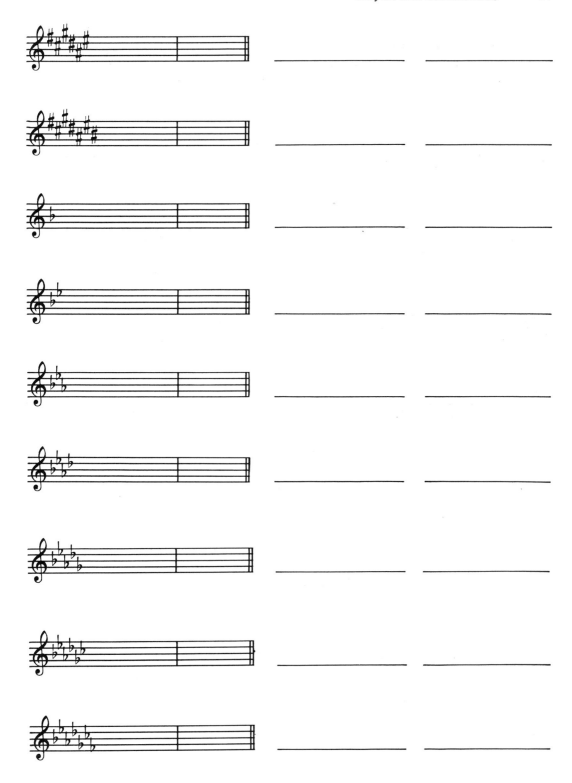

2. Compose four-measure melodies in various major keys. Notate the rhythms and pitches accurately in the treble clef using the appropriate key signatures and time signatures. Draw rhythmic ideas from the exercises in Chapter 2, and construct melodic contours similar to those observed in the music examined in doing the preceding exercise.

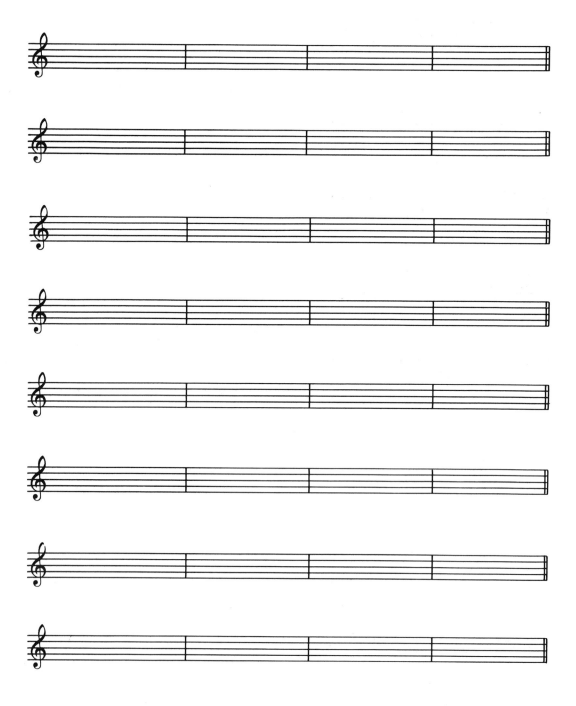

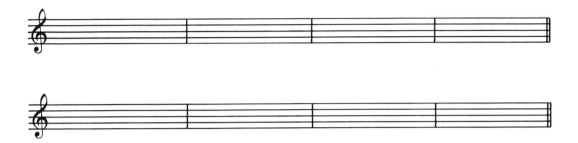

EXERCISES TO PERFORM

1. Play the melodies you wrote for the preceding exercise on the piano or on the instrument you play most proficiently. Revise any rhythm or pitch patterns that sound awkward, unmusical, or uninteresting.
2. Select appropriate melodies in major keys such as those listed for Unprogramed Exercise 1. Play the keynote and sing the pitch with the syllable *do*. If the first note is different from the keynote, play it and sing it with the appropriate syllable. Sing the complete melody with syllables. Play the last note to test whether or not the pitch on which you ended was correct. Repeat each melody in this manner until you can sing the rhythms and pitches accurately and end on the correct pitch consistently.
3. Repeat the procedures of Exercise 2 substituting numbers for the syllables.
4. Repeat the procedures of Exercise 2 using the letter names of the notes. It is not necessary to add "sharp" or "flat" to the letter names of notes that are made sharp or flat by the key signature.

6

Minor Scales and Key Signatures

Minor scales are constructed in three different forms. The lower tetrachords of the three forms are the same, but the upper tetrachords vary according to function. All three forms of minor, like major, are selective seven-tone scales. They differ from major in the location of half steps and, in one form, in the number of half steps. The characteristic feature common to all forms of minor is a half step between the second and third degrees of the scale.

Natural Minor

The *natural minor* scale pattern is produced by the natural notes (without sharps or flats) starting from A and by the white keys of the piano when A is the keynote. Numbered from the keynote, the half steps are between 2 and 3 and between 5 and 6, with whole steps elsewhere.

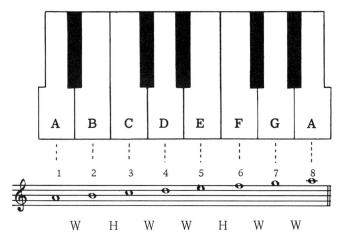

Syllables and numbers are applied to minor scales in two ways. In one system the first note of the scale is 1 or *do* just as in major. In this system the vowel sounds of the syllable names are altered for those notes that differ from the major scale pattern. In the other system the syllable names and numbers of C major are applied to A minor, since both keys have the same signature—no sharps or flats.

A	B	C	D	E	F	G	A
1	2	3	4	5	6	7	8
do	*re*	*me*	*fa*	*sol*	*le*	*te*	*do*
6	7	8–1	2	3	4	5	6
la	*ti*	*do*	*re*	*mi*	*fa*	*sol*	*la*
Keynote							Keynote

The system in which A in A minor is called 1 or *do* assigns the same names to notes in major and minor that have the same functions. For example, the keynote is 1 or *do* and the fifth degree of the scale is 5 or *sol* in both major and minor. This system has many advantages in the study of harmony where the special functions of the various scale degrees are of primary importance. However, the other system, in which syllable and number names are determined by the key signature without reference to whether the mode is major or minor, is used in the public schools and is advocated by the leading elementary music education methods. It is useful to be familiar with both systems and fluent in the one applicable to one's primary interests.

All twelve pitches of the chromatic scale may serve as keynotes of minor scales. For natural minor scales other than the one beginning on A, the proper pattern of half and whole steps is achieved, as with major scales, by the addition of the necessary accidentals or by the use of the appropriate key signature. Of the three forms of minor, only the natural minor is comprised exclusively of the pitches indicated by the key signature.

Harmonic Minor

The harmonic structures traditionally associated with minor are not produced by the notes of the natural minor scale or the key signature. To produce the harmonic structures commonly used in minor, the seventh degree of the natural minor scale, counting up from the keynote, is raised a half step. The resulting scale is the *harmonic minor* scale.

Harmonic minor scales are like natural minor scales in that they have half steps between 2 and 3 and between 5 and 6; in addition they have a half step between 7 and 8, like major scales. In this sense, harmonic minor is a hybrid scale combining elements of minor and major. The interval below the raised seventh tone, which without alteration is a whole step, is enlarged a half step. This interval, equal to a whole step plus a half step, will be identified in this chapter and the next by the symbol W + H.

The key signature is the same for natural minor and harmonic minor. The alteration of the seventh degree in harmonic minor is always accomplished by the use of an accidental rather than by a change in the key signature. The key signature for all forms of the A minor scale is no sharps or flats. In the harmonic form of the A minor scale the seventh degree, G, is raised by a sharp. Both systems of letter and syllable names are adapted to harmonic minor, with modified vowel sounds in the syllables reflecting the chromatic alteration.

	A	B	C	D	E	F	G♯	A
{ 1	2	3	4	5	6	7	8
do	re	me	fa	sol	le	ti	do
{ 6	7	8-1	2	3	4	5	6
la	ti	do	re	mi	fa	si	la
Keynote							Keynote

Melodic Minor

In minor the raised seventh scale degree, which is often used for harmonic reasons, in conjunction with the unaltered sixth degree produces a whole-plus-half interval between 6 and 7. This interval is sometimes avoided in melodic lines by raising the sixth degree of the scale as well as the seventh. The resulting scale pattern, in which both the sixth and seventh degrees are raised a half step from natural minor, is that of the ascending *melodic minor* scale. Its half steps are between 2 and 3 and between 7 and 8. Unlike other scales, the ascending and descending forms of melodic minor differ from each other. The descending form is the same as natural minor, with half steps between 6 and 5 and between 3 and 2. Thus the sixth and seventh scale degrees are a half step higher in the ascending form than in the descending form. Since they are different, both are shown in the example below.

Melodic minor also uses the same key signature as natural minor. The alterations of the ascending sixth and seventh degrees are accomplished by accidentals, which are cancelled in the descending form. Both systems of letter and syllable names are used for melodic minor, with the vowel sounds of the syllables modified in accordance with the varied scale patterns.

	A	B	C	D	E	F♯	G♯	A	G♮	F♮	E	D	C	B	A
{ 1	2	3	4	5	6	7	8	7	6	5	4	3	2	1
do	re	me	fa	sol	la	ti	do	te	le	sol	fa	me	re	do
{ 6	7	8-1	2	3	4	5	6	5	4	3	2	1-8	7	6
la	ti	do	re	mi	fi	si	la	sol	fa	mi	re	do	ti	la
Keynote														Keynote

Abstract minor scale patterns are named and customarily illustrated as they are in the examples in this chapter. Music in minor keys draws freely from all three forms, with the choice for a particular passage dictated by three interrelated factors—underlying harmony, melodic line, and style.

Minor Key Signatures

The key signatures and keynotes are the same for all three forms of minor. Major keys and minor keys use the same key signatures but for different keynotes. The next example shows the relationship between the major and minor keynote associated with each key signature. It is customary, when identifying keys by letters without specifying major or minor, to use capital letters for major and lower-case letters for minor.

When a major keynote is in a space, the keynote of the minor key with the same signature is in the next lower space. When a major keynote is on a line, the keynote of the minor key with the same signature is on the next lower line. Sharps and flats in the signature apply to the keynotes and are essential in identifying the key—for instance, C-sharp minor, B-flat minor.

The signature for a given minor key is the same as that for the major key one space above for keynotes in spaces, and one line above for keynotes on lines. All sharp minor keys except E and B have sharp keynotes. All natural keynotes in minor except A, B, and E and all flat keynotes require signatures with flats.

The major and minor keys with the same signature are *relative* to each other. C-sharp minor is the *relative minor* of E major, and E major is the *relative major* of C-sharp minor. Each major key has its relative minor, and each minor key has its relative major.

The major and minor keys with the same keynote are *parallel* to each other. E minor is the *parallel minor* of E major, and E major is the *parallel major* of E minor. Each major key has a parallel minor, and each minor key has a parallel major.

The key signatures produce the tonal patterns of major and natural minor. Harmonic and melodic minor result from adding one or two sharps or double sharps or cancelling one or two flats. G major and all three forms of its relative and parallel minor are given in the next example for comparison and to illustrate the preceding statements.

Major

Relative Natural Minor

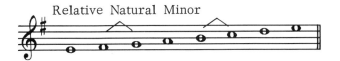

Relative Harmonic Minor

Relative Melodic Minor

Parallel Natural Minor

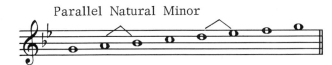

Parallel Harmonic Minor

Parallel Melodic Minor

Double-sharps are required in the harmonic and ascending melodic forms of G-sharp, D-sharp, and A-sharp minor.

Harmonic Minor   Melodic Minor

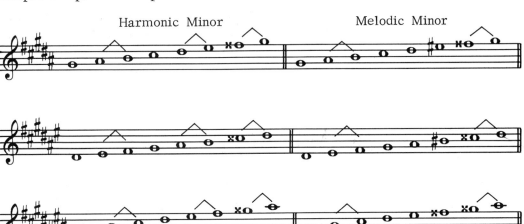

EXERCISES TO WRITE: PROGRAMED

1. The numbers represent scale degrees. Mark the location of the half steps in each of the scale patterns named.

    (a) Major

1	2	3	4	5	6	7	8

1	2	3	4	5	6	7	8

    (b) Natural minor

1	2	3	4	5	6	7	8

1	2	3	4	5	6	7	8

    (c) Harmonic minor

1	2	3	4	5	6	7	8

1	2	3	4	5	6	7	8

    (d) Melodic minor

1	2	3	4	5	6	7	8	7	6	5	4	3	2	1

1	2	3	4	5	6	7	8	7	6	5	4	3	2	1

2. Add sharps or flats as required to make the scales indicated. Mark the half steps.

(a) Natural minor

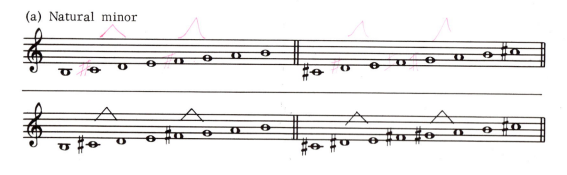

(b) Harmonic minor

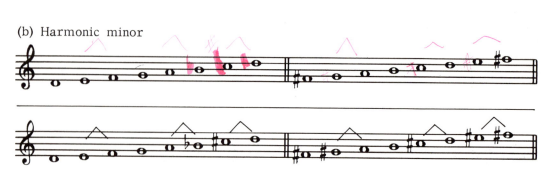

(c) Melodic minor

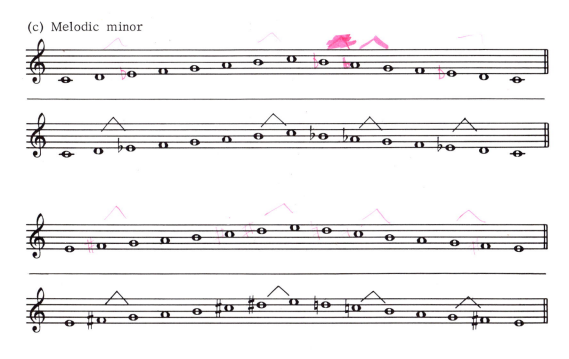

3. Name the minor key indicated by each of the key signatures and write the keynote on the staff. If the keynote occurs in two places within the staff, either octave is correct. Refer to the example on page 74 if you have difficulty.

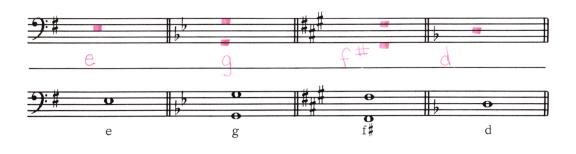

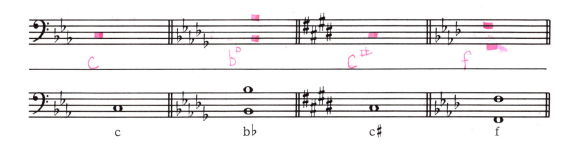

4. Add the proper key signature before each of the following minor keynotes.

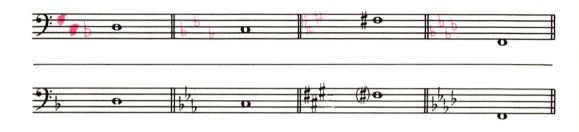

5. The F major scale is given. Using the proper key signatures, write its relative and parallel minor scales in the forms specified. Mark the half steps. If you have difficulty, refer to the examples of the relative and parallel minor scales of G major, on pages 74–75.

Major

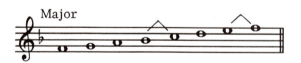

Relative natural minor   Relative harmonic minor

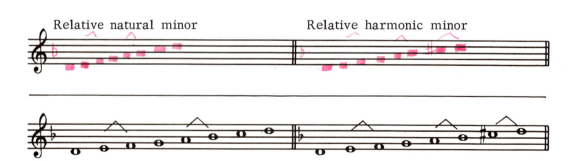

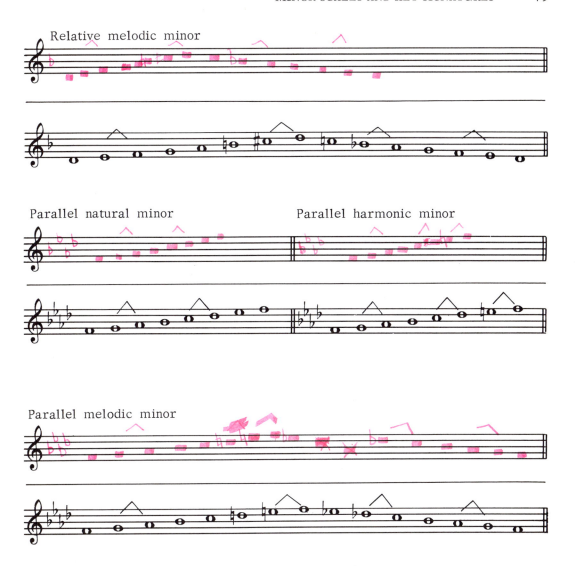

EXERCISES TO WRITE: UNPROGRAMED

1. In the following table minor keys are indicated by lower-case letters in column 1. The number of sharps and flats in the key signature is given in columns 2 and 3. The letter name of the keynote, which ordinarily is the last note of a melody, is given in capital letters in column 5. Find compositions in as many different minor keys as possible. Fill in columns 4, 6, and 7 for compositions in minor keys that are listed. Fill in all columns for compositions in minor keys that are not listed. If the last note of the melody is a note other than the minor keynote, check to be sure that the melody is in a minor key.

Minor key	Sharps	Flats	First note	Last note	Composer or source	Title of composition
a	0	0		A		
e	1			E		
d		1		D		
b	2			B		
g		2		G		
f♯	3			F♯		
c		3		C		
c♯	4			C♯		
f	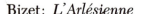	4		F		

2. Select four melodies from those listed in Exercise 1 and copy the first eight measures of each using the proper key signature and time signature. Starting with the keynote, write in ascending order the letter name of each note used in the melody. Indicate whether the form of minor is *natural, harmonic, melodic,* or a combination of these. Circle the letter names of any notes used in the melody that are not in any form of the minor scale, and ignore these in determining the form of minor. The Provençal folk melody used by Bizet in *L'Arlésienne* is given as a model.

Bizet: *L'Arlésienne*

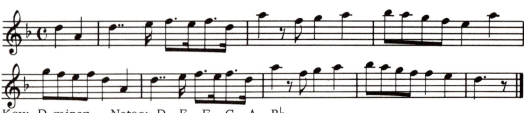

Key: D minor   Notes: D E F G A B♭
Scale: Natural or harmonic minor (C missing)

Key: Notes: Scale:

Key: Notes: Scale:

Key: Notes: Scale:

Key: Notes: Scale:

3. Compose melodies in various minor keys. Notate the rhythms and pitches in the bass clef using the appropriate key signature and time signature. Begin and end some of the melodies with incomplete measures and exploit the resources of all three forms of minor.

EXERCISES TO PERFORM

1. Reading from the examples and written exercises, play all three forms of minor scales on the piano.
2. Without reference to notation, play on the piano or other instrument ascending and descending minor scales. Start on each note of the chromatic scale in turn, and play the three forms of minor in rotation.
3. Using a neutral syllable such as *loo*, sing each form of minor, ascending and descending, from a starting pitch sounded on the piano or other fixed pitch source. Sound the starting pitch again at the end of the scale to see if your ending note is in tune.
4. Using the system prevalent in your sphere of musical activity, sing with syllables each form of minor, ascending and descending.
5. Sing minor scales with letter names, adding "sharp" or "flat" to the letters as required.
6. Listen to major and minor scales being played and distinguish by ear between major and the various forms of minor.
7. Select appropriate melodies in minor keys such as those listed for Exercise 1 in the unprogramed exercises. Play the keynote and sing the pitch with the syllable *do* or *la* (depending upon the system you prefer) or with a neutral syllable such as *loo*. Sing the complete melody with the syllables of your choice. Play the last note to test whether or not the pitch on which you ended was correct. Repeat each melody in this manner until you can sing the rhythms and pitches accurately and end on the correct pitch consistently. Be especially careful to sing correctly the notes that vary in the different forms of minor.

8. Repeat the procedures of Exercise 7 substituting numbers and/or letter names for the syllables.
9. Play the melodies you wrote for Unprogramed Exercise 3 on the piano or on some other instrument for which music is written in the bass clef. Revise any rhythm or pitch patterns that sound awkward, unmusical, or uninteresting.

7

Other
Scales

Major and minor scales provide the tonal basis for most of our familiar music, but there are many other scales, some ancient and some modern.

Church Modes

Prior to the emergence of major-minor tonality, a complete scale system developed. These scales are known collectively as the *church modes*, the *ecclesiastical modes*, or simply as the *modes*. The modes are associated particularly with liturgical music, but secular music, too, was largely derived from modal scale resources until about 1600. A theoretical or historical study of the modes is beyond the scope of this book. However, renewed interest in older music and the persistence of modal influences in newer music dictate consideration of their salient features.

The church modes are most easily understood as seven-tone scales encompassing, between the first note and its repetition an octave higher, five whole steps and two half steps. The pattern of whole steps and half steps is different for each mode. All of the patterns are produced by the natural notes when each note is taken in turn as the starting note of a modal scale. The modal scale patterns and the Greek names by which they are known are given in the following example.

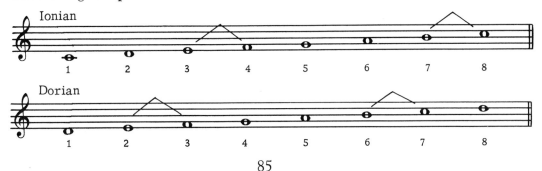

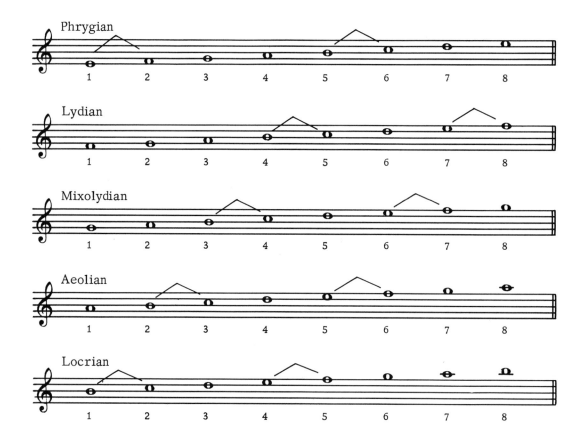

To facilitate comparison, all of the modal scales are shown starting on C in the following example. Observe the flats and sharps required to produce the various modal scale patterns when C is the keynote, or *final* as it is called in modal terminology.

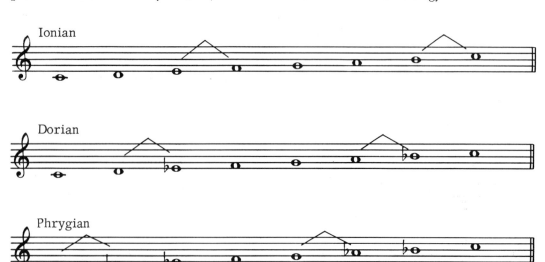

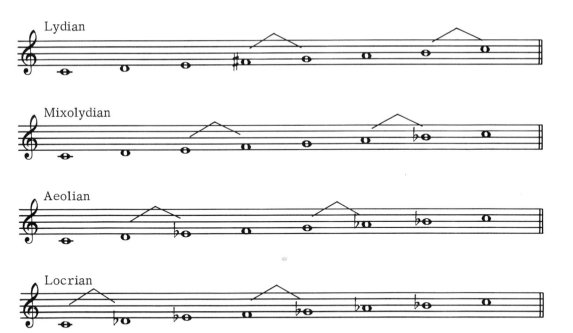

The Ionian and Aeolian modes have the same structure as major and natural minor, respectively. The modal designations for these scale patterns are used only when required by the context. Otherwise they are called simply major or minor. The Locrian mode, which was added to complete the system, exists in theory only, because no satisfactory closing chord is possible with notes derived from it.

The chants of the Catholic liturgy, constituting the largest collection of modal music, use only four modes—Dorian, Phrygian, Lydian, and Mixolydian—plus a variant of each of these for a total of eight. The difference between the four modes and their variants, designated by the prefix *hypo*, is essentially one of range, which is not a consideration in modern scales and multipart music. Books containing these chants identify the mode of each by number, as follows:

I. Dorian	V. Lydian
II. Hypodorian	VI. Hypolydian
III. Phrygian	VII. Mixolydian
IV. Hypophrygian	VIII. Hypomixolydian

Pentatonic Scales

Pentatonic scales, as their name suggests, are five-tone scales. Of all the scales they are the most ancient, having been traced back almost 4,000 years. Pentatonic scales occur in the music of early and primitive cultures and are considered to be the prototypes of all scales. Many five-tone scale patterns are theoretically possible, but pentatonic usually implies some arrangement of the tonal relationships illustrated next.

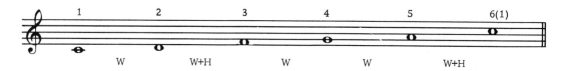

This pentatonic scale has two intervals larger than a whole step and none smaller. No tone in this interval pattern asserts itself strongly as the keynote. Therefore, any tone can function as the keynote, and each produces a pentatonic scale with a unique sequence of intervals.

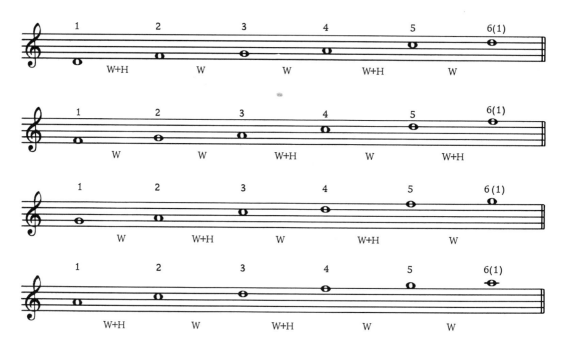

The black keys of a piano produce the pentatonic scale patterns.

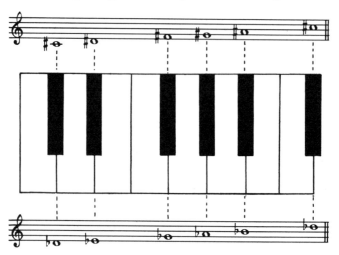

Whole-Tone Scales

Whole-tone scales were first exploited shortly before the beginning of the present century. They are six-tone scales with whole steps between all consecutive notes. Whole-tone scales are produced by alternate notes of the chromatic scale.

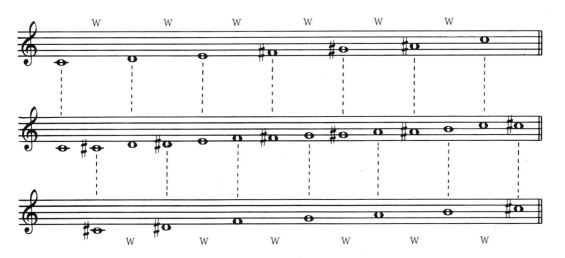

The following example shows these same two whole-tone scales notated enharmonically, using flats instead of sharps.

Each of the whole-tone scales illustrated uses half of the available pitches, and all have the same pattern of equal intervals. Though whole-tone scales can be notated enharmonically and begin (and end) on different notes, their effect is essentially the same. They provide a limited, but occasionally delightful, tonal resource.

Conventional major-minor key signatures are adapted for modal and pentatonic music simply by selecting the key signature which produces the required pitches for the scale pattern or by using a conventional signature for the modal keynote (final) and accidentals as necessary. Accidentals are required in all whole-tone music since no conventional key signature produces a whole-tone scale.

Other scales, both theoretical and practical, exist in the music of our culture, but the only one used extensively is the *twelve-tone* or *duodecuple* scale. *Twelve-tone* and *duodecuple* are terms applied to the all-inclusive scale (otherwise known as the chromatic scale) when all of the notes are treated equally and no tonal center, or tonic, is implied. Twelve-tone music employs serial techniques originally formulated by Arnold Schoenberg. Key signatures are not used in this style which, by nature, abounds in accidentals and enharmonic spellings.

EXERCISES TO WRITE: PROGRAMED

1. Name the church mode produced by the diatonic (natural) notes when scales are played
   starting on:

   C _____   D _____
              Ionian   *Dorian*

       E _____   F _____
                 Phrygian   *Lydian*

   G _____   A _____
              Mixolydian   *Aeolian*

           B _____
                    Locrian

2. Name the mode of the following scales on A written with conventional key signatures.

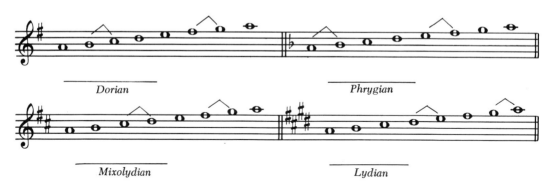

      _____   _____
          Dorian   *Phrygian*

      _____   _____
         Mixolydian   *Lydian*

3. Add sharps or flats to individual notes as required to produce the specified modal scales on
   D and G. Mark the half steps.

Dorian

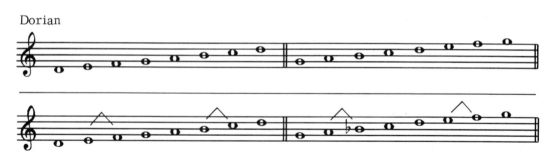

Phrygian

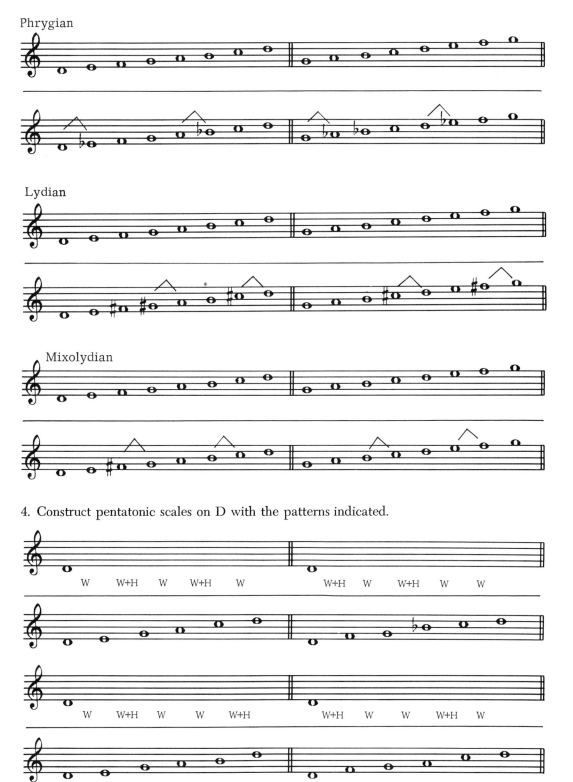

Lydian

Mixolydian

4. Construct pentatonic scales on D with the patterns indicated.

W   W+H   W   W+H   W   W+H   W   W+H   W   W

W   W+H   W   W   W+H   W+H   W   W   W+H   W

5. Add sharps and flats to the notes as required to make whole-tone scales. The same whole-tone scale can be notated in different ways and may include both sharps and flats.

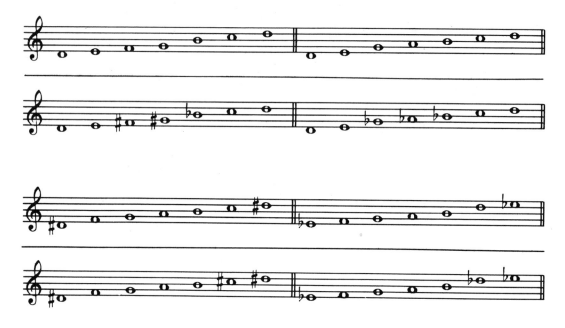

EXERCISES TO WRITE: UNPROGRAMED

1. Compose a short melody in D Dorian. Begin and end on D, and organize the tones so that D is firmly established as the tonal center. Use natural notes (the white keys on the piano) exclusively. The Dorian mode sounds like natural minor with the sixth degree (B) raised a half step. The sixth degree and the seventh degree, which is a whole step below the final (keynote), give the Dorian mode its characteristic sound. Feature these two tones to emphasize the Dorian equality of your melody.

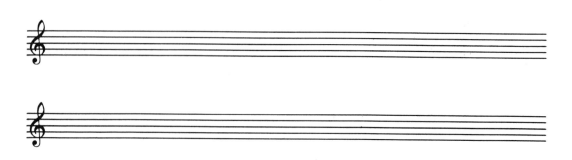

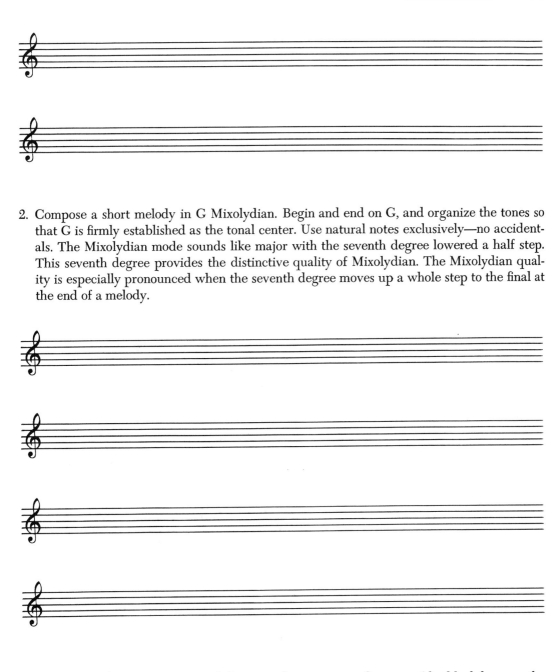

2. Compose a short melody in G Mixolydian. Begin and end on G, and organize the tones so that G is firmly established as the tonal center. Use natural notes exclusively—no accidentals. The Mixolydian mode sounds like major with the seventh degree lowered a half step. This seventh degree provides the distinctive quality of Mixolydian. The Mixolydian quality is especially pronounced when the seventh degree moves up a whole step to the final at the end of a melody.

3. Compose a short pentatonic melody using sharp notes or flat notes (the black keys on the piano) exclusively. Arbitrarily select one of the notes as the keynote; establish it as the tonal center, and end on it.

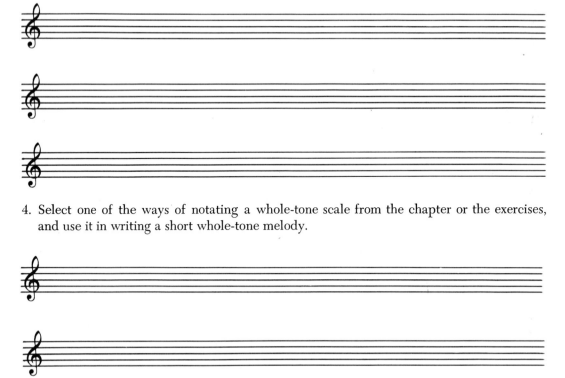

4. Select one of the ways of notating a whole-tone scale from the chapter or the exercises, and use it in writing a short whole-tone melody.

EXERCISES TO PERFORM

1. Play all of the examples and written exercises in the chapter, listening for the distinctive characteristics of each mode and scale. Correct any errors or inadequacies that become apparent when you hear the melodies you composed.
2. When the scales of this chapter are played, identify them by sound.
3. Play on the piano or other instrument any scale selected from this chapter when the starting note is named.
4. When a starting pitch is sounded, sing a matching tone and use it as the first note of any specified scale.

8

Intervals

The difference in pitch between any two notes is an *interval*. Two notes sounded or written in succession create a *melodic interval*. Two notes sounded together, or written one above the other, create a *harmonic interval*.

The basic name for each interval is determined by the number of scale degrees that are spanned by the two notes, including the steps on which both notes appear. The intervals between C and the other notes of the C major scale are:

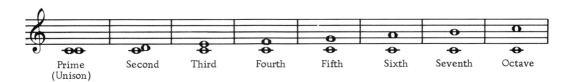

| Prime (Unison) | Second | Third | Fourth | Fifth | Sixth | Seventh | Octave |

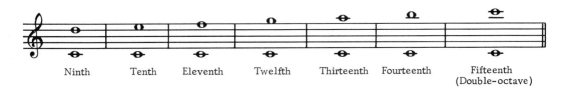

| Ninth | Tenth | Eleventh | Twelfth | Thirteenth | Fourteenth | Fifteenth (Double-octave) |

Intervals that exceed an octave are *compound intervals*. Each compound interval duplicates an interval relationship found within an octave. Compound intervals, especially those larger than a tenth, are commonly designated by their simple names. The interval from C up to G, for example, is usually called a fifth even when the actual interval is a twelfth. Representative intervals within an octave are aligned vertically with corresponding compound intervals in the following example.

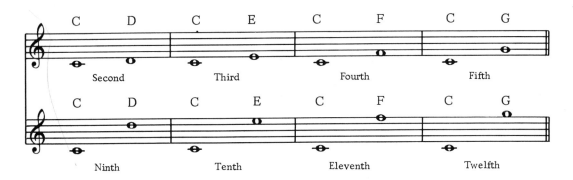

Odd-numbered intervals go from a line to a line or from a space to a space. Even-numbered intervals go from a line to a space or from a space to a line.

The number of scale degrees spanned by an interval gives only the basic name. The *quality* of an interval is determined by the precise number of semitones between the two notes. Interval quality varies with the location of the two notes on the staff and with the sharps and flats applied, but the numerical interval designations are constant regardless of staff position or chromatic alteration.

Interval quality is denoted by the terms *perfect, major, minor, diminished,* and *augmented.* The term *perfect* is applied only to primes, fourths, fifths, octaves, and their compounds. The terms *major* and *minor* are applied only to seconds, thirds, sixths, sevenths, and their compounds. These two groups of intervals are mutually exclusive. No interval in the *perfect* group can be major or minor, and no interval in the *major-minor* group can be perfect. The terms *diminished* and *augmented* are applied to all intervals.

Intervals a semitone smaller than *perfect* are *diminished*. Intervals a semitone larger than *perfect* are *augmented*. Intervals a semitone smaller than *major* are *minor*; those a semitone smaller than *minor* are *diminished*. Intervals a semitone larger than *minor* are *major*; those a semitone larger than *major* are *augmented*. Arranged from small to large, the interval qualities are:

> Diminished——Perfect——Augmented
> Diminished——Minor——Major——Augmented

The first series of interval qualities is used to modify fourths and fifths. It is theoretically correct for primes and octaves as well, but these intervals under ordinary circumstances are perfect. The second series of interval qualities is used to modify seconds, thirds, sixths, and sevenths. Compound intervals are modified in the same way as their counterparts within an octave.

The interval between two tones is decreased when the upper tone is lowered or the lower tone is raised. Conversely, the interval between two tones is increased when the upper tone is raised or the lower tone is lowered. The interval between two tones remains the same when both are raised or lowered the same amount. These principles are illustrated in the following example, which uses a fifth as a representative perfect interval and a third as a representative major-minor interval. The sharps and flats apply only to individual notes.

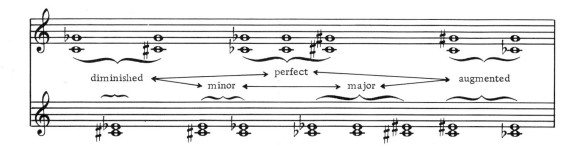

Double-diminished intervals, a semitone smaller than diminished, and *double-augmented* intervals, a semitone larger than augmented, are theoretically possible but are seldom encountered in traditional music.

The number of semitones encompassed by every interval occurring between tones of major and minor scales is given in the next example. The intervals are aligned vertically to show the relationship between each interval and its *inversion*—that is, with one of the notes of the interval transposed an octave to reverse its position as the higher or lower of the pair. The upper note of each interval on the first staff becomes the lower note of its inversion on the second staff, and vice versa.

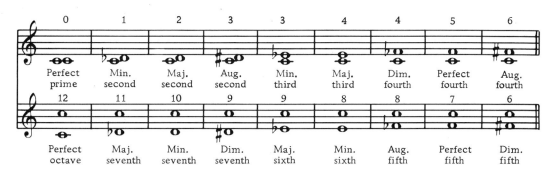

The number of semitones encompassed by any interval and its inversion always totals twelve. The numerical name of any interval subtracted from nine gives the numerical name of its inversion. Observe that:

> Perfect intervals inverted remain perfect.
> Major intervals inverted become minor.
> Minor intervals inverted become major.
> Augmented intervals inverted become diminished.
> Diminished intervals inverted become augmented.

Intervals that encompass the same number of semitones sound the same and cannot be distinguished unless they are seen or associated with a key. The pairs of intervals that have the same sound are:

> Minor thirds and augmented seconds.
> Major thirds and diminished fourths.
> Augmented fourths and diminished fifths.

As written or when associated with a key, these intervals are distinct and must not be confused. As isolated sounds, intervals encompassing three semitones are generally heard as minor thirds and not as augmented seconds. In isolation, the interval encompassing four semitones is invariably interpreted as a major third and not as a diminished fourth. When heard out of context, no such distinction exists between augmented fourths and diminished fifths. They are equally common and indistinguishable by sound alone. *Tritone* (meaning three tones) is another name for an interval spanning six semitones.

Intervals other than those illustrated, such as augmented sixths and diminished thirds, occur in music although they do not appear between components of the conventional scales.

Each scale has not only a characteristic pattern of whole and half steps but a distinctive arrangement of all other intervals as well. The example that follows shows the location by scale degrees of all the intervals in major and the three forms of minor. The intervals at the top are for the scale degrees as shown. The intervals at the bottom are for their inversions. All of the intervals are ascending—the lower note first. The keynote is numbered "1" when it is the lower note of the interval, and "8" when it is the upper note.

INTERVALS:	minor seconds	major seconds	augmented seconds	minor thirds	major thirds	diminished fourths	perfect fourths	augmented fourths
SCALES:								
Major	3–4	1–2		2–4	1–3		1–4	4–7
	7–8	2–3		3–5	4–6		2–5	
		4–5		6–8	5–7		3–6	
		5–6		7–2			5–8	
		6–7					6–2	
							7–3	
Natural Minor	2–3	1–2		1–3	3–5		1–4	6–2
	5–6	3–4		2–4	6–8		2–5	
		4–5		4–6	7–2		3–6	
		6–7		5–7			4–7	
		7–8					5–8	
							7–3	
Harmonic Minor	2–3	1–2	6–7	1–3	3–5	7–3	1–4	4–7
	5–6	3–4		2–4	5–7		2–5	6–2
	7–8	4–5		4–6	6–8		3–6	
				7–2			5–8	
Melodic Minor Ascending	2–3	1–2		1–3	3–5	7–3	1–4	3–6
	7–8	3–4		2–4	4–6		2–5	4–7
		4–5		6–8	5–7		5–8	
		5–6		7–2			6–2	
		6–7						
INTERVALS:	major sevenths	minor sevenths	diminished sevenths	major sixths	minor sixths	augmented fifths	perfect fifths	diminished fifths

In recognizing and constructing intervals, it is helpful to remember that all the notes of a major scale form either major or perfect intervals above the keynote and minor or perfect intervals below the keynote. This principle can be applied to all intervals by arbitrarily thinking of one member as a keynote, whether it is or not. The designations for intervals and qualities may be abbreviated as they are in the next example. The interval is represented by a number and the quality by a preceding letter—"P" for perfect, "M" for major, "m" for minor, "d" for diminished, and "A" for augmented.

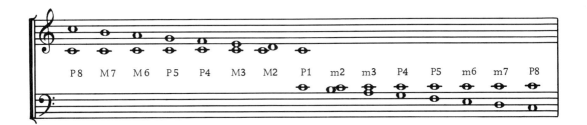

EXERCISES TO WRITE: PROGRAMED

1. Name the intervals, from small to large in order, which can be modified by the quality term *perfect*.

_____, _____, _____, and _____.

   primes (unisons)   *fourths*   *fifths*   *octaves*

2. Name the intervals, from small to large in order, which can be modified by the quality terms *major* and *minor*.

_____, _____, _____, and _____.

   seconds   *thirds*   *sixths*   *sevenths*

3. The quality terms that can be applied to all intervals are:

_____ and _____.

   diminished   *augmented*

4. Give the simple equivalents for these compound intervals:

ninth = _____   eleventh = _____

       second   *fourth*

tenth = _____   twelfth = _____

       third   *fifth*

5. Intervals within an octave are inverted when the lower note is transposed up an octave or the upper note is transposed down an octave.

A second inverted becomes a _____.

      seventh

A third inverted becomes a _____.

      sixth

A fourth inverted becomes a _____.

      fifth

A fifth inverted becomes a _____.

      fourth

A sixth inverted becomes a ____third____ .

third

A seventh inverted becomes a ____second____ .

second

6. Some qualities remain the same when an interval is inverted; others change.
   A perfect interval inverted remains a ____perfect____ interval.

   perfect

   A major interval inverted becomes a ____minor____ interval.

   minor

   A minor interval inverted becomes a ____major____ interval.

   major

   An augmented interval inverted becomes a ____diminished____ interval.

   diminished

   A diminished interval inverted becomes an ____augmented____ interval.

   augmented

7. Between a major keynote and the scale degrees above it the intervals are all either perfect
   or ____major____ .

   major

8. Between a major keynote and the scale degrees below it the intervals are all either perfect
   or ____minor____ .

   minor

9. The total number of semitones encompassed by any interval and its inversion is
   ____twelve____ .

   twelve

10. Name the intervals precisely—interval and quality—using the abbreviations shown on
    pages 98–99.

P8   m7   M6   P5   P4   M3   M2   P1   M2   m3   P4   P5   m6   m7   P8

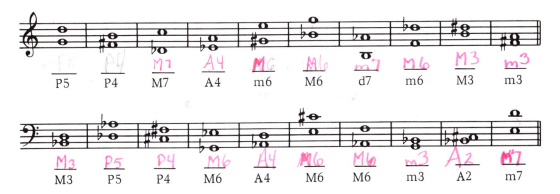

11. Using appropriate abbreviations, name the simple interval which is equivalent to each of the compound intervals.

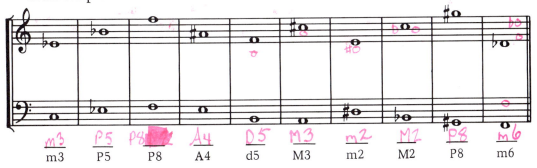

12. Add sharps and/or flats to make the intervals conform to the qualities specified. Spell each interval differently, starting with the lowest spelling for the interval on the left. A note without a sharp or a flat will be regarded as a natural. (For review see page 97.)

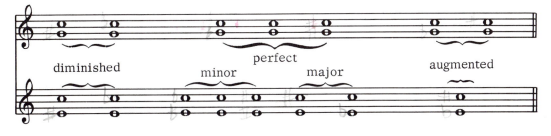

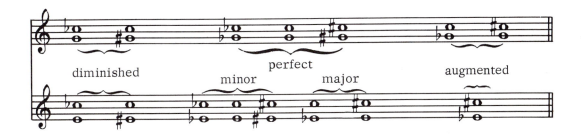

13. Write the specified intervals both below and above the given notes in the manner of the model.

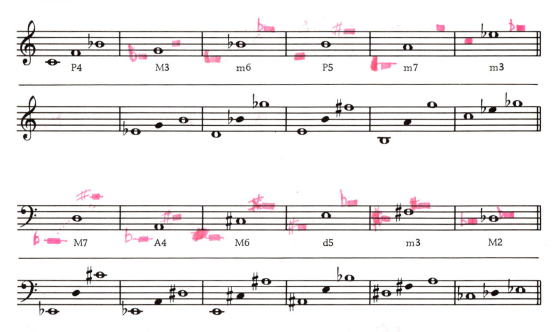

14. In the following exercises the measures with accidentals establish tonal patterns. Continue the patterns adding sharps, flats, and naturals as required to make the specified intervals.

Minor thirds

Major thirds

Perfect fourths

Perfect fifths

Minor sixths

Major sixths

Minor sevenths

Major sevenths

15. Continue the interval analysis, naming precisely the intervals between consecutive notes. Give the simple name for compound intervals.

Humperdinck: *Hansel and Gretel*

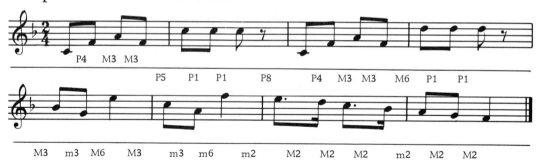

Strauss: *Blue Danube*

EXERCISES TO WRITE: UNPROGRAMED

1. Locate and identify melodies containing a variety of melodic intervals. Copy the melodies and analyze the intervals between consecutive notes.

Composer or source: Title:

EXERCISES TO PERFORM

1. Play the interval patterns of Programed Exercise 14, both with and without reference to the notation. Think of the spelling of the intervals while playing and listen for the distinctive sound of each interval and quality.

2. From a fixed lower tone play all of the intervals melodically (one note after the other) in expanding order from minor second to perfect octave. Then from a fixed higher tone play all of the intervals melodically in contracting order from perfect octave to minor second. Drill until you can recognize each melodic interval by its sound, either ascending or descending.

3. From a fixed lower tone play all of the intervals harmonically (the two notes together) in expanding order for minor second to perfect octave. Then from a fixed higher tone play all of the intervals harmonically in contracting order from perfect octave to minor second. Drill until you can recognize each harmonic interval by its sound.

4. Practice playing all of the intervals, starting from various notes.

5. Practice singing all of the intervals from assigned pitches, both ascending and descending. When the interval to be sung is named and a pitch given, sing the given pitch and then the pitch required to produce the desired interval. Sing intervals with neutral syllables and, when the name of the given pitch is known, with letter names.

6. Take intervals from dictation. When the letter name of one note is given and a melodic or harmonic interval is played, write both notes on the staff and name the interval.

9

Chord

Structures

Three or more notes written vertically or sounded together are a *chord*. Chords consisting of three alternate scale tones are *triads*, the foundation structures of harmony.

Triads

Triads in their most obvious arrangement consist of three alternate scale tones on consecutive lines or in consecutive spaces of the staff.

In this spacing the intervals between adjacent members of triad structures are thirds. The interval between the bottom and top notes is a fifth.

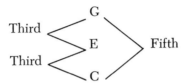

The thirds in triad structures may be major or minor. The fifths are perfect, diminished, or augmented, depending upon the particular combination of major and minor thirds. Chords are always described and constructed from bottom to top—the lowest note or interval first, the highest note or interval last. The possible combinations of major and minor thirds produce four different triad structures:

Major third + minor third = Major triad
Minor third + major third = Minor triad
Minor third + minor third = Diminished triad
Major third + major third = Augmented triad

Major, minor, diminished, and augmented triad structures are represented proportionally in the following diagram. Each crossbar equals a semitone.

Major Triad   Minor Triad   Diminished Triad   Augmented Triad

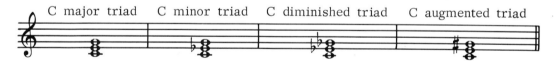

Major and minor triads are constructed of unequal intervals—a major third and a minor third. Diminished and augmented triads are constructed of equal intervals—two minor thirds in the former and two major thirds in the latter.

Triads are in *root position* when all three notes are on consecutive lines or in consecutive spaces. Triads in root position are identified by the letter name of the lowest note, regardless of type.

C major triad   C minor triad   C diminished triad   C augmented triad

The lowest note of triads in root position is the *root*. The other two chord members derive their names from the interval between them and the root. The middle note is the *third*, and the top note is the *fifth*.

The tones of a triad may be rearranged so that the third or fifth is below the root. In any arrangement, the type of triad, its letter name, and the designations of its components remain the same. A chord is in the *first inversion* when the third is the lowest member. A chord is in the *second inversion* when the fifth is the lowest member. Neither the order nor the spacing of the upper notes has any bearing on the inversion. All four types of triads may be inverted. The intervals between notes of inverted triads are a third and a fourth. The upper note of the fourth is always the root.

Root positions   First inversions   Second inversions

For purposes of analysis an inverted triad can be put in root position by the rearrangement of its components so that all three notes are on consecutive lines or in consecutive spaces. In this spacing the root, letter name, and type are most apparent.

Seventh Chords

A *seventh chord* is formed when another third is added to a triad structure. Seventh chords take their name from the interval between this added note and the root of the chord. Both major and minor thirds are added to triad structures as sevenths. Various combinations of major and minor thirds, found as alternate notes of major and minor scales, produce seven different seventh-chord structures. All seven are shown in the next example above the same root, G, for direct comparison. The most systematic method of identifying seventh chords, in the absence of a completely standard terminology, is to specify the type of triad and seventh. In this system a major triad with a minor seventh is called a *major-minor* seventh chord, a diminished triad with a diminished seventh is called a *diminished-diminished* seventh chord, and so forth. These names are somewhat cumbersome, but they provide a basis for concise and explicit abbreviations. Musicians commonly use functional or descriptive names for all but the infrequently heard *minor-major* and *augmented-major* seventh chords. Associate the seventh-chord structures in the example with their type names, abbreviations, and common names.

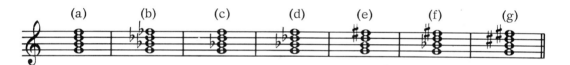

Chord Type	Abbreviation	Common Name
(a) Major-minor seventh	Mm7	Dominant seventh
(b) Diminished-diminished seventh	dd7	Diminished seventh
(c) Minor-minor seventh	mm7	Minor seventh or Secondary seventh
(d) Diminished-minor seventh	dm7	Leading-tone seventh or Half-diminished seventh
(e) Major-major seventh	MM7	Major seventh
(f) Minor-major seventh	mM7	
(g) Augmented-major seventh	AM7	

Only the first four of the seventh chord structures shown are included in the harmonic resources of traditional music. Of the four, the first is used the most and the fourth the least.

The principles and procedures are much the same for both triads and seventh chords. Both take their letter names from the roots. The four chord members in seventh chords, reading up from the root, are: *root, third, fifth,* and *seventh.* In any arrangement these designations are constant. A seventh chord is in the *first inversion* when the third is the lowest member; it is in the *second inversion* when the fifth is the lowest member, and in the *third inversion* when the seventh is the lowest member. The root position and the three inversions of the G dominant seventh chord (Mm7) are shown below. The second and third inversions are written down an octave to avoid leger lines.

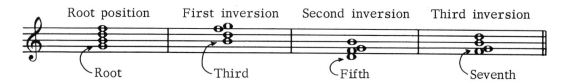

Root position   First inversion   Second inversion   Third inversion

Root   Third   Fifth   Seventh

Other Chord Structures

The harmonic vocabulary of most composers was limited to major, minor, and diminished triads and to the four most common types of seventh chords until the latter part of the nineteenth century, although there were some notable earlier excursions into more exotic tonal combinations. The beauty and scope of traditional musical expression is all the more amazing with these restricted tonal resources. In more recent times composers have combined tones with uninhibited freedom to produce a broad spectrum of harmonic color.

The process of building chords in thirds was extended by adding another third above the seventh. The note a third above the seventh is a ninth above the root, and chords so constructed are called *ninth chords*. Both major and minor ninths are added to seventh chords. Most often the seventh chord underlying the ninth is of the dominant (major-minor) type shown.

Dominant major ninth   Dominant minor ninth

Ninth chords are used mainly in root position and occasionally in the third inversion. Other inversions are less satisfactory.

The process of building chords in thirds led inevitably to the next third, the *eleventh*. Perfect and augmented elevenths added to major and minor ninths produce *eleventh chords*. These are most often heard in root position.

Eleventh chords

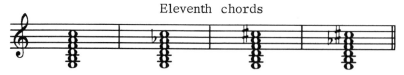

The augmented eleventh chords contain notes not available in any one major or minor scale. Requiring notes beyond those of a conventional scale is no longer recognized as a barrier in the construction of chords.

The ultimate alternate scale tone structures are *thirteenth chords*. Diatonic thirteen chords, like the one shown, contain every note of a major scale. Another third above the thirteenth would duplicate the root two octaves higher. An almost infinite number of thirteenth-chord types are possible by adding various combinations of sharps and flats to their seven different notes, but thirteenth chords are too involved to be practical. They are used occasionally as novelties and as the culminating harmony of pyramiding thirds.

Thirteenth chord

Seventh, ninth, eleventh, and thirteenth chords can be simplified—often without impairing their effectiveness, and sometimes improving it—by omitting one or more tones. Chords conceived in this manner may be called *chords of omission*. A few of the many possibilities are illustrated below.

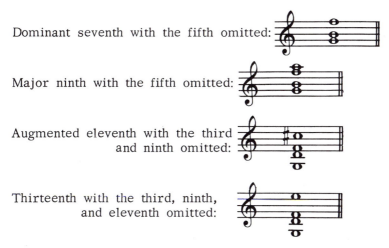

Dominant seventh with the fifth omitted:

Major ninth with the fifth omitted:

Augmented eleventh with the third and ninth omitted:

Thirteenth with the third, ninth, and eleventh omitted:

The pungency of simple triads and seventh chords can be increased by adding one or more tones to their basic structures. Chords constructed in this way are known as *added note chords* or *chords of addition*. Although their name belies the fact, they are closely related to the chords of omission. Added notes are identified by their interval relationship with the root of the chord to which they are added. The most frequent additions to triads are illustrated in the following examples.

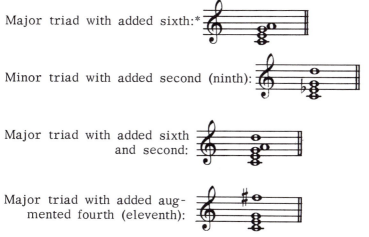

Major triad with added sixth:*

Minor triad with added second (ninth):

Major triad with added sixth and second:

Major triad with added augmented fourth (eleventh):

The process of addition includes the possibility of adding one complete chord to another and of combining two forms, such as major and minor, of the same chord. Sonorities that result from combining two or more chords or chord forms are called *polychords*. Major triads with roots an augmented fourth apart and seventh chords with both major and minor thirds are two of the most useful and most frequently used of the polychords.

* Also may be analyzed as a mm7 in the first inversion.

C major combined with F-sharp major:

C seventh with both major and minor thirds:

Polychords are not so remote from conventional chord structures as they appear to be at first glance. Every seventh chord contains the elements of two triads; every ninth chord contains the elements of three triads and two seventh chords, etc. The polychord designation, however, is reserved for chord combinations with more remote relationships and fewer common tones.

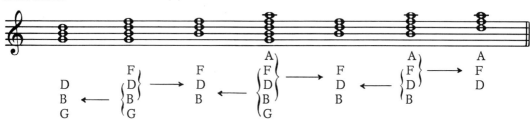

Chords are also constructed currently of intervals other than thirds. Chords built in seconds, fourths, and fifths have been and continue to be used in the twentieth century. *Non-tertial* is the classification for such chords. In comparison with the triads and seventh chords of conventional music, they both look and sound strange, but they are all part of the musical vocabulary of our time.

Chord in seconds (cluster)   Chord in fourths   Chord in fifths

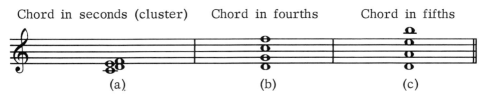

(a)   (b)   (c)

Like conventional chord structures, nontertial chords can be expanded, contracted, inverted, and rearranged, and by these means they sometimes acquire a more traditional shape and sound. The chords below have the same notes as the corresponding chords of the previous example.

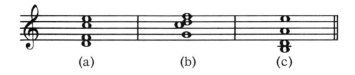

(a)   (b)   (c)

EXERCISES TO WRITE: PROGRAMED

1. Identify the type of triad by writing "M" for major, "m" for minor, "d" for diminished, and "A" for augmented below the chords.

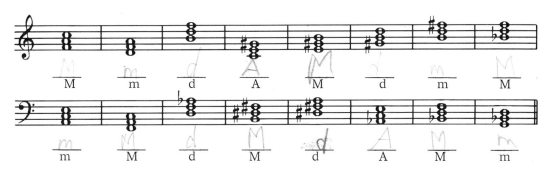

2. Write the designated triad structures above the given roots.

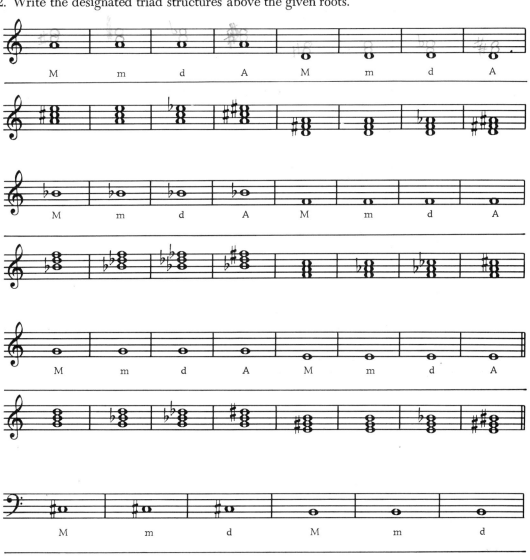

3. Write the designated seventh chords above the given roots.

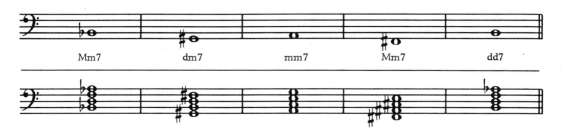

4. Write the chords described on the given roots.
   (a) A thirteenth chord with the notes of an A major scale.
   (b) An augmented eleventh chord with a major ninth and the most usual seventh chord structure.
   (c) A major triad with an added second (ninth) above an added sixth.
   (d) A dominant minor ninth with the fifth omitted.
   (e) A major-minor seventh chord with a minor third (tenth) added above.
   (f) A three-note chord in perfect fourths.
   (g) A four-note chord in perfect fifths.
   (h) A dominant seventh chord with the third omitted.

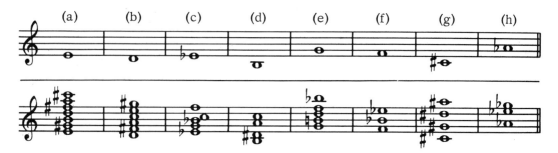

EXERCISES TO WRITE: UNPROGRAMED

1. Describe the following chords. Some may be analyzed in more than one way.

(a)

(b)

(c)

(d)

(e)

(f)

(g)

(h)

2. Write an example of each type of contemporary chord specified. Experiment at the piano to discover interesting and useful combinations of tones. After you have written the chords, describe them in the space at the right.

Ninth chord

Eleventh chord

Thirteenth chord

Chord of addition

Chord of omission

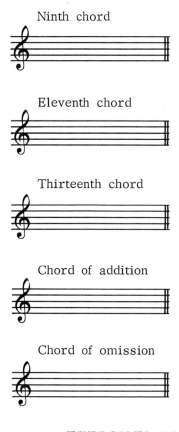

EXERCISES TO PERFORM

1. Name the types of triads outlined when the pitches of various triad structures are played in succession.
2. Name the types of triads heard when various types of triads are played in root position and in the two inversions.
3. Sing the outline of all major and minor triads starting from a given pitch as root, third, or fifth.
4. Identify the type and write the complete triad on the staff when the root is named and a triad played.
5. Name the lowest sounding member (root, third, or fifth) when major and minor triads are played.
6. Identify by type the dominant (Mm7), diminished (dd7), secondary (mm7), and half-diminished (dm7) seventh chords when they are played.
7. Name the lowest sounding member in each chord when dominant seventh chords are played in root position and in the three inversions.

10

Chord Symbols and Names

Symbols and names have been devised for the various chords as aids in teaching and understanding music. Chord symbols have also been developed partially to overcome the tedium of writing and the expense of printing music, especially that for keyboard and certain string instruments that play chords. Some of the common chord symbols and names used in place of, in conjunction with, or in addition to conventional notation are explored in this chapter.

Roman Numerals

One system of chord symbols, shown below, represents chords by expressing the scale degree of their roots in Roman numerals. This system shows the relationships within a key that are associated with chord function in the study of harmony. In minor keys, the harmonic form of minor is ordinarily used for chords.

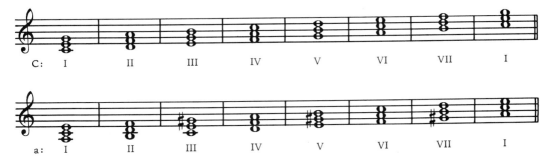

The next example shows a refinement of this system, which distinguishes the four types of triads. The minor form of the numeral followed by a degree sign is used for diminished triads. The major form of the numeral followed by a plus sign is used for augmented triads.

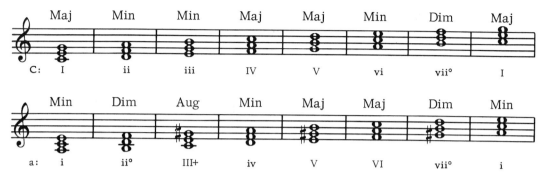

A triad symbol followed by a "7" indicates a seventh chord. The four seven-chord structures found in traditional music are shown next, with appropriate symbols on the scale degrees where they occur in major and harmonic minor. The 7 following major and minor triad symbols indicates the addition of a minor seventh above the root. The 7 following a diminished triad symbol indicates the addition of a diminished seventh above the root. The degree sign with a diagonal line through it between a Roman numeral and a 7 indicates the addition of a minor seventh to a diminished triad. The symbol reflects the actual chord structure regardless of whether the notes are in the key or changed by accidentals.

Names and Classifications

Chords are identified by names as well as by numbers. The chord names reflect the functions of the chords and/or the relationship of their roots to the keynote and to the chord built on the keynote, the *tonic* chord.

Scale Degree	Chord Symbol	Chord Name
1	I	Tonic
2	II	Supertonic
3	III	Mediant
4	IV	Subdominant
5	V	Dominant
6	VI	Submediant
7	VII	Subtonic** or Leading tone

The names given for chords are also used for the corresponding notes of the scale; for example, the first degree of the scale is the tonic note, and the chord built on it is the tonic chord; the fifth degree of the scale is the dominant note, and the chord built on it is the dominant chord.

* Sometimes written vii°7°, in which case the diagonal line is omitted from the degree sign in the diminished-minor seventh chord symbol.

**Subtonic is sometimes used exclusively for the note and chord a whole tone below the tonic, in which case *leading tone* is used for the note a semitone below the tonic and for the chord built on it.

The tonic, both note and chord, is the center of its particular tonal universe. The other notes and chords of the key gravitate toward it. Compositions normally begin and end with a tonic chord, and melodies normally end on the tonic note. To the tonic exclusively belongs the quality of complete repose. No harmonic progression achieves complete finality until it comes to rest on the tonic chord. In this sense, all other chords are subservient to it.

Second in importance to the tonic and directly contrasting with it is the dominant. The qualities of action and tension are inherent in the dominant. It creates a demand for resolution that is satisfied by progression to the tonic. The designations for the others notes and chords of a key describe their relationship to these two poles—tonic and dominant.

The subdominant is the same interval (a perfect fifth) below the tonic as the dominant is above. The mediant is midway between the dominant and the tonic. The submediant is midway between the subdominant and the tonic. The supertonic is directly above the tonic. The subtonic is directly below the tonic. The note a half step below the tonic is also called the *leading tone* because it leads to the tonic, and chords built on it are called leading tone chords. These relationships, with the tonic as the central tone, are shown graphically in the following diagram.

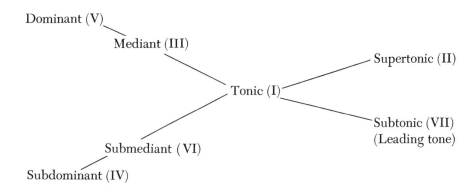

Dominant (V)
Mediant (III)
Supertonic (II)
Tonic (I)
Subtonic (VII)
(Leading tone)
Submediant (VI)
Subdominant (IV)

Here the notes of C major are arranged in the pattern of the diagram:

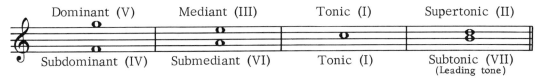

Dominant (V)   Mediant (III)   Tonic (I)   Supertonic (II)
Subdominant (IV)   Submediant (VI)   Tonic (I)   Subtonic (VII)
(Leading tone)

The names of the chords are the same in major keys and minor keys. The next example shows the triads of C major and C natural minor. Chord qualities are reflected in the Roman numeral symbols.

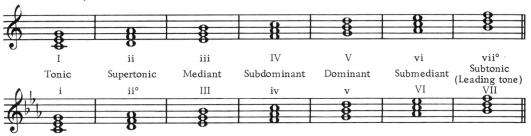

I	ii	iii	IV	V	vi	vii°
Tonic	Supertonic	Mediant	Subdominant	Dominant	Submediant	Subtonic (Leading tone)
i	ii°	III	iv	v	VI	VII

The tonic triad and the triads built on roots a fifth above and a fifth below the tonic are the *primary triads*. The three primary triads are the basic components of tonal harmony. They are:

Tonic (I)
Dominant (V)
Subdominant (IV)

The primary triads are major in major keys and minor in natural minor. In a major key and its parallel minor, the chord roots are the same.

The remaining, or *secondary triads,* are:

Supertonic (ii)
Mediant (iii)
Submediant (vi)
Subtonic or leading tone (vii°)

The secondary triads, in addition to providing harmonic interest and variety, substitute for a primary chord with which they share two tones. Functionally, the subtonic or leading tone triad is so closely identified with the dominant seventh chord that it is often regarded as an adjunct of that chord rather than as a separate entity. The secondary triads of C major are shown following the primary triads with which they are associated and for which they may be substituted.

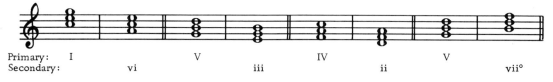

Primary: I   V   IV   V
Secondary: vi   iii   ii   vii°

Figured Bass

During the baroque era (c. 1600–1750), a system for representing chords by Arabic numerals was used. This system showed the relationship of the upper tones to the lowest note, or bass, rather than to a key. A bass with these numbers is a *figured* or *thorough bass.* The numbers represent intervals above the bass. In the example that follows, the note G is taken in turn as the root, third, and fifth of a triad and as the root, third, fifth, and seventh of a seventh chord. The letter name of the root is given above the chord. The complete figuration according to figured bass principles is given below the chord. The notes represented by the numbers in parentheses were taken for granted in the absence of any indication to the contrary, so in practice these numbers were not included in the figuration unless they required an accidental.

G	E	C	G	E	C	A
(5)	6	6	7	6	(6)	(6) *
(3)	(3)	4	(5)	5	4	4
			(3)	(3)	3	2

The normal figured bass for G triads in root position, first inversion, and second inversion and for G seventh chords in root position, first, second, and third inversions is shown with the proper chord member in the bass:

* In this figuration the "4" is sometimes omitted also.

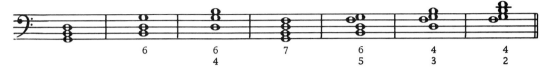

Thus the meanings of the figures, which represent intervals above the bass note, are:

$\begin{matrix}(5)\\(3)\end{matrix}$—the bass tone is the root of a triad

6 —the bass tone is the third of a triad

$\begin{matrix}6\\4\end{matrix}$ —the bass tone is the fifth of a triad

7 —the bass tone is the root of a seventh chord

$\begin{matrix}6\\5\end{matrix}$ —the bass tone is the third of a seventh chord

$\begin{matrix}4\\3\end{matrix}$ —the bass tone is the fifth of a seventh chord

$\begin{matrix}4\\2\end{matrix}$ —the bass tone is the seventh of a seventh chord

Tones that are not chord members are indicated, as are chord tones, by Arabic numerals showing the interval above the bass.

In the figured bass system, notes are in the key and in accordance with the key signature unless otherwise indicated. A sharp, flat, or natural preceding or following a number indicates a corresponding alteration of the note represented by the number. A sharp, flat, or natural alone—that is, not associated with a number—applies to the note a third above the bass. Sometimes a diagonal line through a number or some similar mark is used in place of a sharp or natural sign to indicate that a tone is to be raised a half step. Here is the figured bass for some typical altered chords (chords containing notes modified by accidentals):

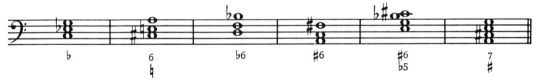

Baroque keyboard players were adept at improvising and could provide an elaborate accompaniment with full harmonies from a simple figured bass line. Playing from a figured bass—or *realizing* a figured bass, as it is called—is almost a lost art, but the figured bass numbers are combined with Roman numeral chord symbols in many current harmony textbooks.

The Roman and Arabic numerals combined provide more complete information about a chord than does either one independently. The Roman numerals show the relationship of the chord to the key and provide clues to its function. They can be modified to show chord structure. The Arabic numerals indicate inversions. Together they tell everything about a chord except its spacing and doubling. The combined figuration is given for all of the diatonic triads and common seventh chords in major. The example is in C, but the figuration would be the same in any major key. One of the advantages of chord symbols is that they are constant, whereas chord spellings are different in every key.

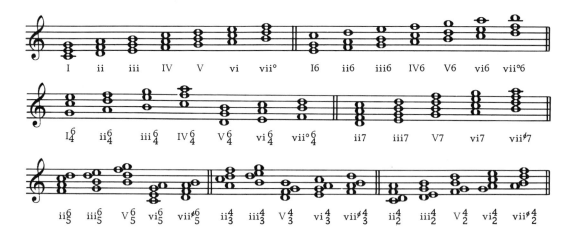

Symbols in School and Recreational Songs

School music series and community and recreational song collections often provide chord symbols either above a single melodic line or in addition to a piano accompaniment. The symbols are given as an aid in providing an accompaniment for the song on a piano or a guitar or on some instrument designed especially for classroom use, such as an Autoharp. The harmonic backgrounds of such songs generally are simple, and the chord symbols required are few. Only three types of chords are available on Autoharps—major triads, minor triads, and dominant sevenths—and these in just a few keys.

In this system a major triad is indicated by the letter name of its root. A minor triad is indicated by the letter name of its root followed by the letter "m" or "min." A dominant (major-minor) seventh chord is indicated by the letter name of its root followed by a figure "7."

C = C major triad
Cm = C minor triad
C7 = C dominant seventh chord

Other chord structures, which are rare in this style, are indicated by the same symbols used in jazz and popular music. The chord symbol tells only which notes to include in the harmony. The choice of inversion, spacing, doubling, and rhythm, other than total duration, is left to the discretion of the performer.

Jazz and Popular Chord Symbols

The chord symbols used in jazz and popular music are the same type as those used in school and recreational music, but the scope of the system is greatly expanded to accommodate more varied harmonic structures. The symbols are not completely uniform in all publications, but the principles are standard.

A letter stands for a major triad with that note as the root. When the root is flat or sharp, the flat or sharp is added to the letter name even if it is in the key signature.

The twelve major triads shown are the foundation of jazz harmony. Modifications and additions are reflected in the symbols. Enharmonic spellings are used freely, and flats are preferred.

Minor, augmented, and diminished triads are indicated by adding one of the following to the letter name:

> minor: m, occasionally min or mi
> augmented: +, occasionally aug
> diminished: dim, rarely °

The diminished triad symbol normally implies a diminished seventh chord, so no "7" is used in the figuration of diminished chords.

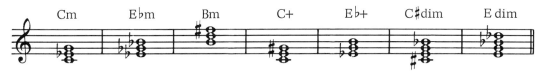

Major sixths above the root, indicated by the figure "6," are added to major and minor triads; thus:

A "7" following a triad symbol indicates the addition of a minor seventh. Minor sevenths are added to major, minor, and augmented triads and to a major third-diminished fifth structure that does not occur as a traditional triad. The symbols used for the various seventh chord structures are given above the notation in the example. The plus sign indicating that the fifth is to be augmented is found in the three locations illustrated. A minus sign or a flat sign before the number shows that the fifth is to be lowered a half step.

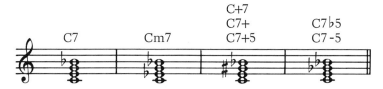

There are only three different diminished seventh chord sounds, each of which can be spelled enharmonically four ways. In jazz figuration any chord member or the enharmonic of any chord member may be used with the abbreviation *dim* to show which of the three diminished seventh chords is to be played. The more probable symbols are given for each chord.

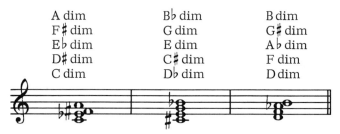

Major sevenths are usual only with major triads. The symbol for this chord has the abbreviation *maj* between the letter name and the seven:

Ninth chords are signified by the figure "9." The basic structure consists of a dominant seventh (Mm7) chord plus a major ninth. This and other possible ninth chord structures are:

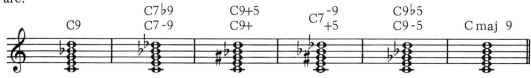

The numbers "11" and "13" appear occasionally in chord symbols, indicating the addition of these intervals above the note specified by the letter name. Eleventh and thirteenth chords are rarely played complete, so the actual structure varies with the performer and the performance. Elements essential to create a dominant seventh sound are generally included in these chords. Other components are optional. Incomplete chords are the equivalent of chords of omission, but there are no symbols for them.

Notes, other than the sixth, to be added to chord structures are indicated by the usual symbol plus the letter name of the added note, thus:

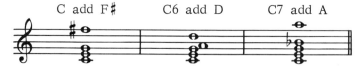

EXERCISES TO WRITE: PROGRAMED

1. Give the Roman numeral figuration for the chords in the major keys indicated by the key signatures. Modify the symbols to show the exact structure of the chords.

2. Give the Roman numeral figuration for the chords in the minor keys indicated by the key signatures, modifying the symbols to show chord structure as in Exercise 1.

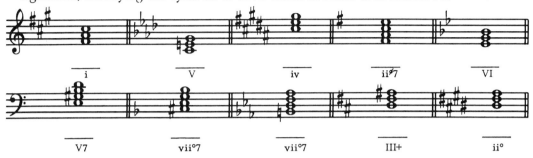

3. Write the specified chords in the major keys denoted by the key signatures. Place the chords as near the center of the staff as possible.

4. Write the specified chords in the minor keys denoted by the key signatures, as in Exercise 3.

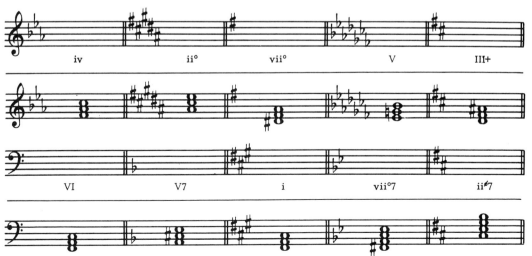

5. Write the Roman numeral symbols (in numerical order) for the primary triads showing their structure in major and harmonic minor.

Major: _____

                  I   *IV*   *V*

Minor: _____

                  i   *iv*   *V*

6. Write the Roman numeral symbols as in Exercise 5 for the secondary triads in major and harmonic minor.

Major: _____

         ii   *iii*   *vi*   *vii*°

Minor: _____

        ii°   *III+*   *VI*   *vii*°

7. Write the primary triads in the major keys denoted by the key signatures. Place the chords as near the center of the staff as possible.

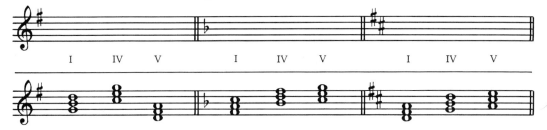

8. Write the secondary triads in the major keys denoted by the key signatures, as in Exercise 7.

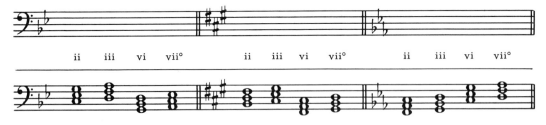

9. Write the primary triads in the minor keys denoted by the key signatures, as in the previous exercises.

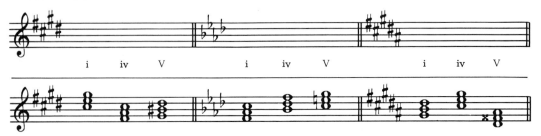

10. Write the secondary triads in the minor keys denoted by the key signatures, as in the previous exercises.

ii°   III+   VI   vii°   ii°   III+   VI   vii°   ii°   III+   VI   vii°

11. Write the figured bass below the chords.

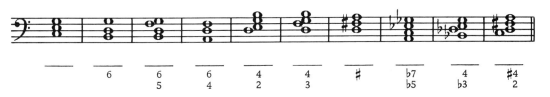

6   6   6   4   4   #   ♭7   4   #4
         5   4   2   3   ♭5   ♭3   2

12. Complete the chords above the figured bass.

6   7   6   #6   ♭5   6   4   ♭7   4
                  #   4   5   2   3
                                                              #

13. Write the chords in the major keys and the inversions indicated. Construct the chords above bass notes within the staff.

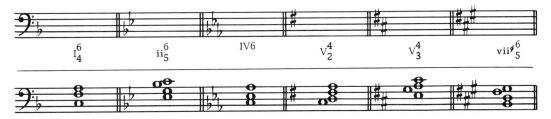

I⁶₄   ii⁶₅   IV6   V⁴₂   V⁴₃   vii⁰⁶₅

14. Write the chords as in Exercise 13 in the minor keys and the inversions indicated.

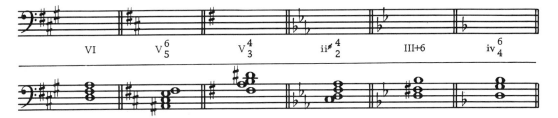

VI   V⁶₅   V⁴₃   ii⁰⁴₂   III+6   iv⁶₄

15. Write the symbols used in school and recreational music above the chords. Remember that inversions do not affect the symbols and that the roots of inversions are the upper notes of the fourths in triads and the upper notes of the seconds in seventh chords.

| F | Dm | C | G7 | Ab | F#m | A7 | Gm | Bm | C7 |

16. Write in root position the chords indicated by the symbols, starting on or below the middle line of the staff.

| Cm | E | G7 | Bm | D | A7 | B | Gm | C7 | F |

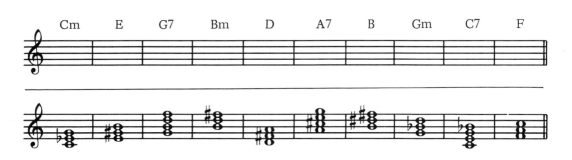

17. Write the symbols used in jazz and popular music above the chords.

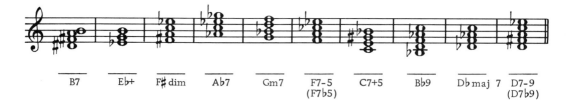

| B7 | Eb+ | F# dim | Ab7 | Gm7 | F7-5 (F7b5) | C7+5 | Bb9 | Db maj 7 | D7-9 (D7b9) |

18. Write in root position the chords indicated by the symbols without using leger lines above the staff.

| Eb6 | E7 | Gm7 | B dim | G aug | C7-9 | Em6 | F9+5 | A maj 7 | B7 |

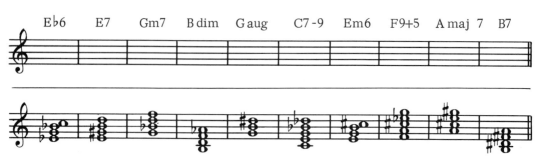

EXERCISES TO WRITE: UNPROGRAMED

1. Select a song from a school music series or from a recreational song book in which chord symbols are given. Copy the melody in the treble clef with the key and time signatures on the staff and the chord symbols above. Add the key and time signatures to the bass staff and draw continuous bar lines through the two staffs. Then, write on the bass staff the chords indicated by the symbols.

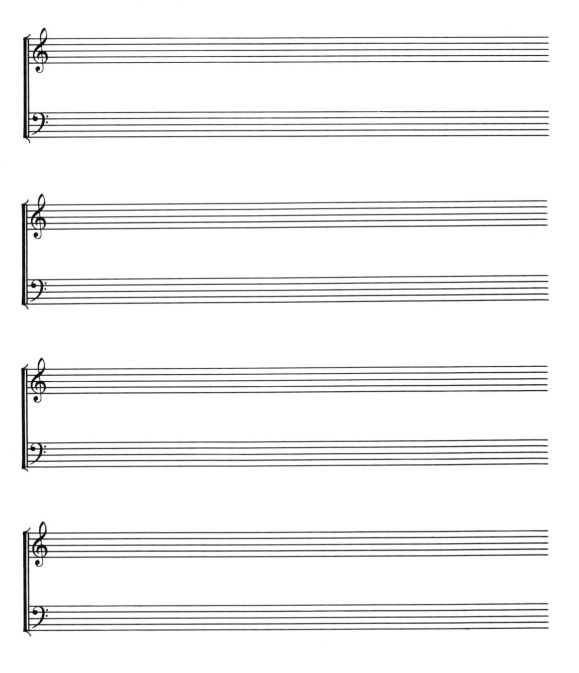

2. Select a popular song and follow the procedures outlined for Exercise 1.

EXERCISES TO PERFORM

Play the following exercises on the piano. If your piano facility is limited, start slowly and play the chords in the simplest manner. More advanced pianists should play the exercises rhythmically, with proper regard for chord spacing and chord connection.

1. Play the examples and written exercises in the chapter, associating the sound of each chord with its symbol and figuration.
2. Play the primary triads in the keys of G, F, D, and B-flat major.
3. Play the secondary triads in the same keys as Exercise 2.
4. Play the primary triads in the keys of A, E, D, and G minor.
5. Play the secondary triads in the same keys as Exercise 4.
6. Play the chords indicated by the symbols in selected familiar songs.
7. Play the chords indicated by the symbols in selected popular songs.

11

Chord Spacing and Doubling

The principles of chord spacing and doubling are most efficiently illustrated and practiced in four parts with ranges corresponding to the four voice classifications—soprano, alto, tenor, and bass.

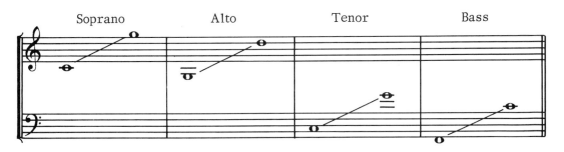

These limits are exceeded in writing for trained voices and for instruments, but they serve as practical guides in the study of chord spacing and doubling. Within the specified vocal ranges, innumerable distributions of chord components and many varied harmonic effects are possible.

Spacing

Other factors being equal, it is desirable to have relatively even distribution of the parts in corresponding registers of the various voices. Unevenly spaced chords characteristically have the smaller intervals between the three upper voices. Intervals exceeding an octave are avoided between the soprano and alto and between the alto and tenor but not between the tenor and bass.

135

Chord spacing is classified as *close* or *open*. A chord is in *close position* when the interval between the soprano and the tenor is less than an octave. A chord is in *open position* when the interval between the soprano and the tenor is an octave or more. The two types of spacing are equally useful.

Close position   Open position

Doubling

Triads in four parts have one note doubled—that is, a note that appears in the chord twice, usually in different octaves. Any note of a triad may be doubled, but composers tend to avoid certain doublings and to favor others. The following is a summary of common practices in doubling.

Doublings avoided:
  Leading tones
  Chromatically altered notes
  Sevenths, ninths, etc.

Doublings preferred, roughly in order of precedence:
  First, fourth, and fifth degrees of the scale
  The fifth (bass) of chords in second inversion
  The root (bass) of chords in root position
  The soprano (root or fifth) of chords in first inversion

These principles will be applied consistently in the examples and exercises in this chapter, but strict conformity in music literature is not to be expected.

All possible bass-soprano relationships for major and minor triads are illustrated with acceptable doubling and spacing in the next example. Numbers above the staff show the chord member in the soprano. Numbers below the staff show the chord member in the bass. Arrows point from the bass to the doubled note when the root or fifth is in the bass and from the soprano to the doubled note when the third is in the bass.

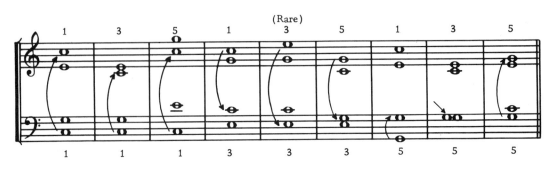

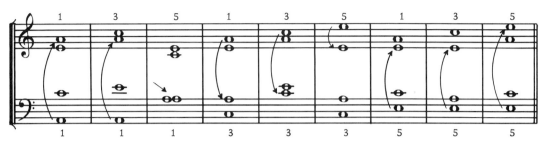

Major and minor triads sometimes are represented by two notes, most often by the root and third, less frequently by the root and fifth or the third and fifth. At cadence points the tonic triad commonly has the third in the alto or tenor and the root tripled in the other three parts. Elsewhere and in other incomplete triads, which are just intervals with chord function, the choice and distribution of notes are less predictable. The accompanying example shows typical incomplete tonic triads in C major and A minor.

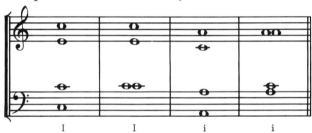

Diminished triads usually are in the first inversion with the third (bass) doubled as shown next. Less often the fifth is doubled. The roots of diminished triads are not doubled as a rule, because they are leading tones or chromatic notes, except in the supertonic in minor.

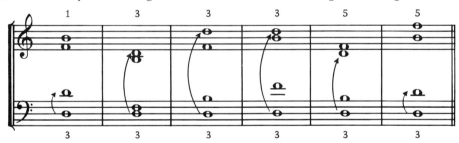

In augmented triads (which are used infrequently) the root or third is doubled, because the fifth invariably is a chromatically altered note. The augmented mediant triads of A minor, F minor, and C-sharp minor, illustrated, have the same basic sound. The spelling and doubling are adjusted according to the key.

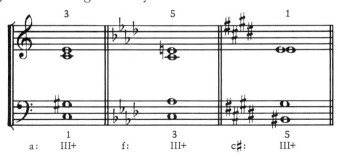

Seventh chords are spaced in accordance with the same principles as triads, but doubling is unnecessary when writing seventh chords in four parts. The distribution of the parts shown for dominant (major-minor) seventh chords in the next example is suitable for all types of seventh chords. Bass-soprano relationships are illustrated as for triads except that, without doubling, the note in the bass cannot also be in the soprano.

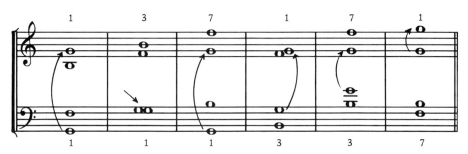

Seventh chords may have the root doubled and the fifth omitted as shown in the following example. This is common in dominant-type seventh chords, less common in other types. The omission of the third is exceptional but possible.

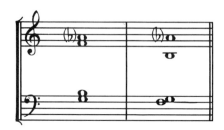

Ninth chords are uncommon in traditional four-part music, and relatively few arrangments of their components are exploited. Typically the root is in the bass, the ninth in the soprano, and the fifth is omitted. Occasionally the seventh is in the bass, the ninth in the soprano, and the fifth omitted. Both of these possibilities are illustrated.

The principles outlined for spacing and doubling in four parts are valid, with minor adjustments, for chords in three and in more than four parts. With fewer parts, spacing tends to be more open, and there are more incomplete chords. With more parts, spacing is generally closer, and the amount of doubling multiplies with each additional part. The proportionate weight assigned to each chord component, however, is relatively constant.

Chord distributions comparable to those advocated for vocal music are also used with good effect in instrumental music. Other distributions are employed for technical reasons, such as keeping chords within the reach of the hands when writing for keyboard instruments, and for variety. Chords are rhythmically motivated in accompaniment patterns, and their components may be sounded in succession rather than simultaneously.

EXERCISES TO WRITE: PROGRAMED

1. Analyze the type of chord, the spacing, and the doubling in the following composition. Write "C" under chords in *close position;* "O" under chords in *open position.* Below the "C" or "O" write the number of any chord member that is doubled or (in incomplete triads) tripled. In the line below the numbers write the abbreviation for the type of complete chords—M, m, A, d, Mm7, etc.—or "inc" for incomplete chords (represented by the root and third). Disregard notes in parentheses in your analysis.

Schumann: *Choral (Album for the Young, No. 4)*

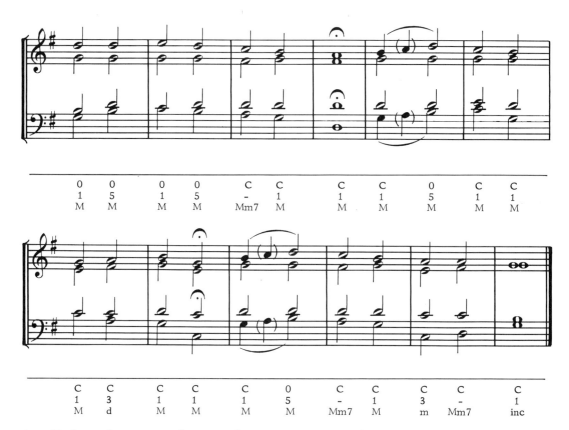

0	0	0	0	C	C	C	C	0	C	C
1	5	1	5	-	1	1	1	5	1	1
M	M	M	M	Mm7	M	M	M	M	M	M

C	C	C	C	C	0	C	C	C	C	C
1	3	1	1	1	5	-	1	3	-	1
M	d	M	M	M	M	Mm7	M	m	Mm7	inc

2. Add alto and tenor parts between the given soprano and bass parts to complete the major triads in close position. Observe strictly the principles of doubling stated in the chapter. The numbers above the soprano and below the bass show the chord members.

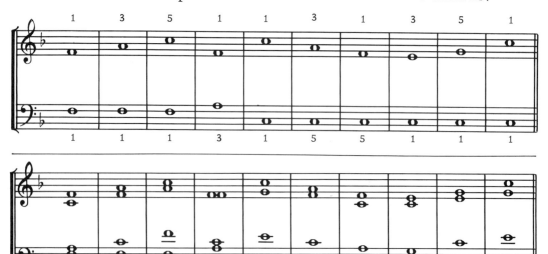

3. Add alto and tenor parts between the given soprano and bass parts as in Exercise 2, to complete the major triads in open position.

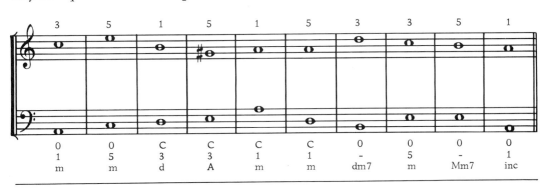

4. Add alto and tenor parts to complete the specified chord structures. Spacing and doubling are indicated below the bass as follows:

O = Open position   m = Minor triad
C = Close position   d = Diminished triad
1 = Root doubled   A = Augmented triad
3 = Third doubled   dm7 = Diminished-minor seventh chord
5 = Fifth doubled   Mm7 = Major-minor seventh chord
– = No note doubled   inc = Incomplete triad (root and minor third)

The chord member in the soprano is shown by numbers above the treble staff. Accidentals may be required in the added parts.

EXERCISES TO WRITE: UNPROGRAMED

1. Write four-part major triads using each bass note successively as root, third, and fifth. Vary the spacing and doubling but conform to the principles outlined in the chapter. Write the number of the chord member in the soprano above the staff and draw an arrow from the bass or soprano to the doubled note. In this exercise and those that follow, notes written with sharps or flats (which would be in the key signature if one were used) may be doubled.

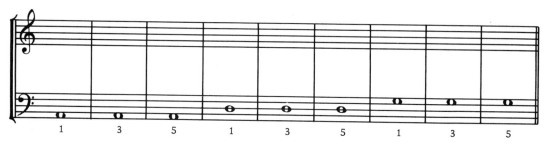

2. Following the procedures described for Exercise 1, write four-part minor triads using each bass note successively as root, third, and fifth. Doubling in minor triads is less circumscribed than in major triads. Any member of a minor triad may be doubled under proper conditions.

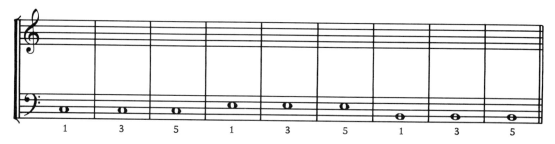

3. Write first inversions of diminished triads on the given bass notes. The preferred doubling is the third (bass). The fifth may be doubled but not the root.

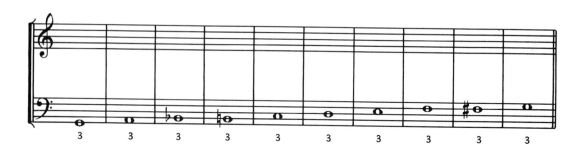

4. Write the augmented triads indicated.

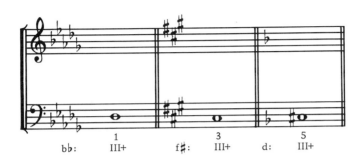

bb: III+   f♯: III+   d: III+
      1   3   5

5. Write complete major-minor (dominant) seventh chords using the given bass note as root, third, fifth, or seventh as indicated.

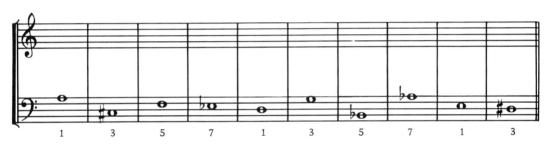

1   3   5   7   1   3   5   7   1   3

6. Write diminished (diminished-diminished) seventh chords on the given roots. Vary the spacing.

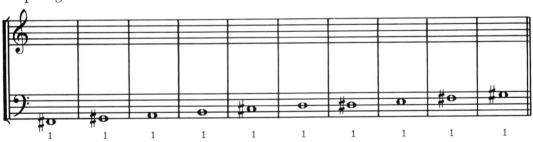

1   1   1   1   1   1   1   1   1   1

7. Analyze the chord structures, spacing, and doubling in selected passages of music in four-part vocal style.

EXERCISES TO PERFORM

These exercises, like similar exercises in previous chapters, should be played on the piano with the performance level geared to the keyboard proficiency of individual students.

1. Play the examples and exercises in this chapter, listening to the quality of each chord and to the effect of the various spacings, doublings, and bass-soprano relationships.
2. Play major and minor triads with proper doubling in close position (one note in the left hand and three in the right) on bass notes assigned as root, third, or fifth.

3. Play diminished triads as in Exercise 2 on bass notes assigned as thirds.
4. Play major and minor triads with proper doubling in open position (two notes in each hand) on bass notes assigned as root, third, or fifth.
5. Play dominant (major-minor) seventh chords in four parts on bass notes assigned as root, third, fifth, or seventh.
6. Play chords as in Exercises 2, 4, and 5 when the assigned note is in the soprano. Select an appropriate bass note, which will determine the inversion.
7. When major, minor, diminished, and augmented triads and major-minor seventh chords are played in open and close position, identify the chord type.
8. When major and minor triads are played:
   (a) Name the inversion or identify the bass as root, third, or fifth.
   (b) Identify the soprano as root, third, or fifth.
9. When major-minor seventh chords are played, respond as in Exercise 8, adding sevenths as possible bass and soprano tones.
10. When major and minor triads and major-minor seventh chords are played in four parts, identify the chord type by an appropriate abbreviation. Write the number of the chord member in the soprano above the abbreviation and the number of the chord member in the bass below the abbreviation.
11. When the letter names of the roots of chords played in Exercise 10 are given, write the chords on the staff in four parts. It is not necessary to hear the alto and tenor as individual notes. They can be filled in according to the principles of spacing and doubling when the type, root, bass, and soprano are known.

Note: Diminished and augmented chords are omitted from certain isolated chord dictation exercises because of the difficulty in recognizing specific members in chords of equal intervals, that is, all minor thirds or all major thirds.

12

Performance Terms and Symbols

Musical scores contain, in addition to pitches and rhythms, many directions for performance. These convey to performers the composer's intentions regarding speed, style, dynamic level, and mood. Italian is the international language of music, and most of the terms are of Italian origin. Words from other languages, with a few exceptions, are associated with the music of a particular country. Most performance terms are indicative or relative rather than precise; they only point the way to authentic interpretation, which ultimately rests with the performer.

The more usual terms are categorized in this chapter. Modifying words and phrases, less common terms, and literal definitions are given in the glossary.

Tempo Indications

The *tempo* is the rate of speed in music. Tempo is most accurately expressed in terms of the number of beats per minute. A *metronome* capable of establishing exact tempos in a wide range was perfected by Johann Maelzel in 1816. Modern versions of the instrument can be set at selected rates to mark from 40 to 208 beats per minute.

The perception of the beat in music is somewhat subjective, and there seems to be an innate tendency to relate the rhythmic flow of music to a norm that perhaps has a physiological basis. Tempos that approximate this norm—around 84 beats per minute—seem most natural. Those that deviate decidedly from it are perceived as either slow or fast. Beyond certain flexible limits the inclination is to divide slow beats and to combine fast beats to bring them within the normal range. The point at which this happens, being subjective, varies with individuals and circumstances, but the perceived beat of music is only infrequently slower than 48 per minute or faster than 156. The beat indicated by the time signature, however, often exceeds this range.

Tempos related to Maelzel's metronome are shown by the abbreviation M.M., or M., or simply by the note representing the beat followed by an equal sign and a number. Thus M.M. $\quarternote = 60$ indicates 60 quarter notes per minute or one per second, and $\halfnote = 120$ indicates

145

120 half notes per minute or two per second. The note representing the beat in the metronome marking does not always agree with that indicated by the time signature. For example, a metronome mark for an eighth note or a dotted half note might be given with a 3/4 time signature. In such cases, conductors normally conduct, and performers feel, the eighth or dotted half note as the beat, rather than the quarter indicated by the signature.

Composers give two figures, such as 112–108, to allow some latitude in the tempo, or they insert the abbreviation *c.* (circa) before the number to show that it is only approximate.

Before the invention of the metronome a tempo terminology evolved which persists to the present time. Its Italian words and phrases lack the precision of metronome markings, but they convey impressions of style as well as pace. Often a metronome mark is combined with an Italian expression to secure the advantages of both methods.

The basic Italian tempo terms are listed in order below, along with diminutive and superlative forms. These cannot be equated with metronome markings. The rates assigned to the various terms on certain metronome scales are completely unrealistic. Those shown in the example reflect the norm and extremes discussed, but even these are only approximate and somewhat arbitrary. The range of beats per minute between an average pace and the slowest is much less than between an average pace and the fastest. In terms of beats per minute, the difference between 84 and 156 is double the difference between 48 and 84.

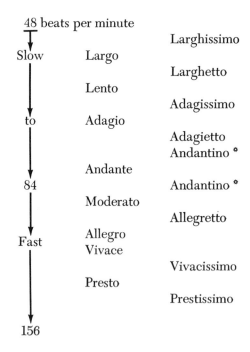

The metronome marks and the tempo terms given in the preceding chart specify a steady pace. Italian words and phrases used to direct variable speeds and changes of tempo are shown next.

---

* *Andantino* is either a little faster or a little slower than *andante,* depending upon whether *andante* is classified as a fast or slow tempo. There is no general agreement, and it has been interpreted both ways. If the mean tempo is placed between *andante* and *moderato,* as shown, then *andante* is on the slow side, and *andantino* is a little faster.

Increase the Tempo

Gradually	Immediately
accelerando (accel.)	*doppio movimento*
affrettando	*piu mosso*
incalcando	*piu moto*
incalzando	

Decrease the Tempo

Gradually	Immediately
allargando (allarg.)	*meno mosso*
calando	*meno moto*
rallentando (rall.)	*ritenuto*
ritardando (rit.)	
slargando	
slentando	
tardando	

Without Measured Tempo	Return to Established Tempo
ad libitum (ad. lib.)	*a tempo*
a piacere	*tempo I*
rubato	*tempo primo*
senza misura	

Dynamic Marks

The signs and symbols denoting intensity of sound are *dynamic marks*. Six, or sometimes eight, degrees of loudness are recognized in music. Dynamics are indicated by the abbreviations almost to the exclusion of the words.

Louder ——————————————————————————————→

Word:	*pianissimo*	*piano*	*mezzo piano*	*mezzo forte*	*forte*	*fortissimo*	
Abbreviation:	*(ppp)*	*pp*	*p*	*mp*	*mf*	*f*	*ff* *(fff)*

←—————————————————————————————— Softer

The *triple-piano* and *triple-forte* abbreviations are used occasionally for exaggerated soft and loud effects.

There are words with abbreviations and signs for gradually increasing or decreasing sound intensity.

crescendo (cresc.) ——————————————— gradually louder

decrescendo (decresc.) ———————————— gradually
diminuendo (dimin.) ————————————→ softer

The following dynamic markings are used on single notes or chords:

forte-piano (fp). A loud attack, then immediately soft.
forzando (fz). Forced. Vigorously accented.
sforzando (sf or *sfz)*. Same as *forzando*.
rinforzando (rf, rfz, or *rinf)*. Reinforced. A sudden stress.

Other Signs and Symbols

Repeat from the beginning.

Repeat the passage between the two signs.

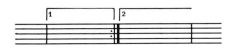

Repeat, omitting the measure(s) of the first ending on the repetition.

Repeat from the beginning. In the *da capo*, repeat signs are ignored.

Repeat from the beginning, ending at *fine* or where the sign appears over a double bar.

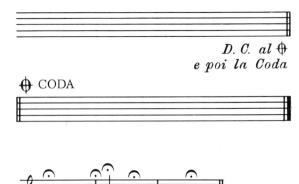

Repeat from the beginning to the sign, and then skip to the coda.

The duration of the note, chord, or rest under the sign is increased, often approximately doubled, at the discretion of the performer. The sign over a bar line signifies a momentary interruption of the rhythm except when it is used to mark the end of a work after a D. C. or D. S. The sign is called a *fermata* or *hold*.

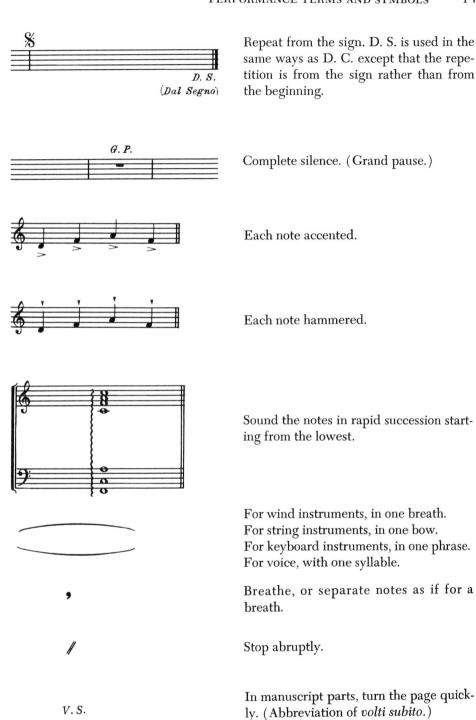

Repeat from the sign. D. S. is used in the same ways as D. C. except that the repetition is from the sign rather than from the beginning.

Complete silence. (Grand pause.)

Each note accented.

Each note hammered.

Sound the notes in rapid succession starting from the lowest.

For wind instruments, in one breath.
For string instruments, in one bow.
For keyboard instruments, in one phrase.
For voice, with one syllable.

Breathe, or separate notes as if for a breath.

Stop abruptly.

In manuscript parts, turn the page quickly. (Abbreviation of *volti subito.*)

Not printed, but written by players in orchestral parts to signal particularly tricky spots.

WRITTEN   PLAYED

as fast as possible, unmeasured

EXERCISES TO WRITE: PROGRAMED

1. The international language of music is _____.

Italian

2. The Italian word used in music for rate of speed is _____.

tempo

3. A device used to establish tempos in music is a _____.

metronome

4. Modern metronomes can be set to tempos as slow as 40 beats and as fast as 208 beats per

_____.

minute

5. The simplest way to indicate precisely a tempo of 72 quarter-note beats per minute is:

_____.

♩ =72

6. The simplest way to indicate precisely a tempo of 104 half-note beats per minute is:

_____.

𝅗𝅥 =104

7. The initial letters of the basic Italian tempo terms (excluding diminutive and superlative forms) are given in order from fast to slow. Complete the words:

P_____, V_____, A_____, M_____,

presto   *vivace*   *allegro*   *moderato*

A_____, A_____, L_____, L_____

andante   *adagio*   *lento*   *largo*

8. The diminutive term meaning slightly faster (less slow) than largo is _____.

larghetto

9. The superlative term meaning slightly slower than adagio is _____.

adagissimo

10. The term which may mean either slightly slower or slightly faster than andante is

_____.

andantino

11. The diminutive term meaning slightly slower than allegro is _____.

allegretto

12. The superlative term meaning faster than presto is _____.

prestissimo

13. Write the standard abbreviations for the dynamic terms below the words:
fortissimo,   forte,   mezzo forte,   mezzo piano,   piano,   pianissimo.

ff	*f*	*mf*	*mp*	*p*	*pp*

14. The abbreviation D.C. means repeat from the _____.

beginning

15. The abbreviation D.S. means repeat from the _____.

sign

EXERCISES TO WRITE: UNPROGRAMED

1. Copy and define every performance term and symbol found in a substantial work of standard music literature for your instrument or voice or for a group with which you perform.

2. From various types of music, compile a representative list of initial tempo markings. Arrange them from the slowest to the fastest according to the pattern of the example on page 146, and give the literal and a descriptive definition of each.

3. Find several works that have both Italian tempo indications and metronome marks. Copy the tempo terms and the metronome marks associated with them. Then discuss the following questions:
   (a) Do the metronome marks seem to agree with the implications of the Italian terms?
   (b) Are different metronome marks associated with the same term?
   (c) What is the range of tempo terms and metronome marks from the slowest to the fastest?

EXERCISES TO PERFORM

1. Establish a tempo of 84 beats per minute with a metronome, if one is available. If not, count at various rates until 84 even beats fit in a minute measured by the second hand on a watch or clock. Tempos can be verified more quickly by doubling the number of beats counted in 30 seconds or multiplying by four the number counted in 15 seconds.
2. After you have established a tempo of 84 beats per minute, sing or play a piece at this tempo. Does it seem slow, fast, or average to you?
3. Play, sing, or listen to music of various tempos. Estimate the metronome mark and write it down during the performance. Determine the correct metronome mark as in Exercise 1 and compare it with your estimate.
4. Compare the tempos of recorded performances with the metronome marks printed in the music. Do concert artists adhere closely to the metronome marks given by composers and editors?

Glossary-Index

Absolute music–Music without literary, dramatic, or pictorial connotations.
A cappella –For unaccompanied voices (literally, for the chapel).
  A cappella choir–A group that performs music without accompaniment.
Accelerando (accel.)–Accelerating; increasing in tempo. *147*
Accidental–A sharp, flat, natural, double-sharp, or double-flat not in the key signature. *31*
Accompaniment (accomp.)–A subsidiary, supporting part in a composition.
Acoustics–The science of sound.
Action–The mechanism of instruments.
Adagietto–Slightly faster than adagio. *146*
Adagio–Leisurely, slow. *146*
Added sixth–A note a sixth above the root added to a triad. *113*
Ad libitum (ad. lib.)–At will. Leaves to the performer's discretion (1) variations from strict tempo
    or (2) the inclusion or omission of a part. *147*
A due–Directs two instruments to play the same part.
Aeolian–One of the church modes. *86, 87.*
Affettuoso (affett.)–With affection, warmth.
Affrettando (affrett.)–Hurrying. *147*
Agitato–Agitated; in an excited manner.
Alberti bass–An accompaniment played by the left hand on a keyboard instrument in which chord
    tones alternate in a fixed pattern.
Al fine–To the end. *148*
Alla–Like, in the manner of. To the, in the, or at the.
Alla Breve–Often called cut time. Simple duple time with the half note as the beat. *17*
Allargando (allarg.)–Decreasing in tempo and, usually, increasing in loudness. *147*
Allegretto–Cheerful, lively. Not quite so fast as allegro. *146*
Allegro–Cheerful, lively, brisk, rapid. *146*
All'ottava (8 –––– or 8va ––––)–Above the notes: play an octave higher. Below the notes: play an
    octave lower. *35*
All'unisono–Play in unison.
Alteration–Changing the pitch by means of a sharp, flat, or natural.
Altered chord–A chord with one or more notes foreign to the key.
Alto–The low female voice or the corresponding part in instrumental music. *135*
  Clef–The C clef with C on the third line of the staff. *33, 34*

155

Amabile—Lovable, tender.

A mezza voce—With half voice; subdued tone.

Amore—Amorously.

Anacrusis—Upbeat. *22*

Andante—Going along, flowing. A tempo midway between fast and slow. *146*

Andantino—Diminutive of andante meaning either a little slower or a little faster than andante. *146*

Animato—With animation, spirit.

A piacere—At pleasure; without measured tempo. *147*

Appassionato—With passion.

Arco—Bow. With the bow.

Aria—Song with instrumental accompaniment.

Arpeggio—The tones of a chord played in succession.

Arrangement—The adaptation of a composition for performance by a medium other than the one for which it was conceived.

Assai—Very.

Asymmetric meter—Meter in which measures are divided asymmetrically, causing irregular spacing of the secondary accents. *16–17, 18*

A tempo—Return to established tempo. *147*

Atonal, atonality—Without tonality; not in a key.

Attacca—Proceed to the next section or movement without pause.

Augmentation—Increasing, usually doubling, the rhythmic value.

Augmented interval—A half step larger than perfect or major. *96*

Authentic cadence—Harmonic progression V to I as a cadence.

Autoharp—A string instrument played by strumming, on which simple chords are played by depressing a bar. *124*

Bar, bar line—A vertical line across a staff to divide measures; "bar" is also used sometimes as a synonym for "measure." *15*

Barbaro—Barbaric, ferocious.

Baritone—The male voice lower than tenor but higher than bass, or an instrument with related range.

Baroque—The period of music between 1600 and 1750.

Bass—The low male voice or a corresponding instrument or part. *135*

    Clef—The F clef with F on the fourth line. *33, 34*

Basso continuo—The bass line with figures indicating the chords to be played.

Basso ostinato—Obstinate bass; a bass figure repeated over and over.

Beam—A heavy line connecting stems of notes in rhythmic groups, taking the place of flags. *3–4, 8*

Beat—The pulse of music; the rhythmic unit to which one responds in marching or dancing and which is marked by the conductor's gestures. *5–6*

Bel—A unit of loudness. A decibel, one-tenth of a bel, represents the smallest variation in loudness detectable by the human ear.

Bizet—L'Arlésienne. *80*

Blue Danube—Strauss. *106*

Bravura—Boldness.

Brillante—Brilliant, showy.

Brio, con—With fire, vigor.

Buffo—Comic, burlesque; a comic singer or part in an opera.

Cacaphony—Bad sound; disorganized and discordant.

Cadence—A harmonic, melodic, or rhythmic formula used at the ends of phrases, sections, movements, and complete works to convey the impression of conclusion.

Cadenza (cad.)—An unaccompanied virtuoso passage in improvisatory style.

Calando (cal.)—Decreasing in tempo and loudness. *147*

Calmando, calmato (calm.)—Calm.

Calore, con—With warmth.

Cantabile (cantab.), cantando, cantante—Singable or in a singing style.

Cantus firmus—A pre-existent melody used in polyphonic composition.

Capo, da—From the beginning. *148*

Capriccioso—Capriciously.

C clef—A clef sign that fixes the location of middle C; it appears on the third and fourth lines of the staff in modern notation. *33–34*

Cent—A scientific unit for measuring differences in pitch, equal to 1/100 of a tempered semitone.

Chamber music—Instrumental music for small groups of performers with one on a part.

Choral—Schumann. *139–140*

Chord—Three or more tones sounding together. *109–114*
    of Addition—113–114
    Eleventh—112
    Inversion—110, 111–112
    Jazz and Popular—124–126
    Names—120–122
    Ninth—112
    Nontertial—114
    of Omission—113
    Polychords—113–114
    School and Recreational—124
    Seventh— 111–112, 120
    Structure—109–114
    Symbols—119–120, 122–126
    Thirteenth—112
    Triads—109–110, 119–120

Chromatic note—A note that is foreign to the key written with an accidental.

Chromatic scale—A twelve-tone scale with half steps between all successive tones. *47–48*

Church modes—The scales of early music, especially sacred monody, and of medieval and renaissance music theory. *85–87*

Circa (c., ca.)—Approximately, about. *146*

Circle of fifths—When notes an interval of a perfect fifth apart are taken in succession, the one following the twelfth has the same letter name as the first. *58–59*

Classic—Denotes the period of music roughly from 1750 to 1825. Also, music in a related style or form.

Clavier—A keyboard, or any keyboard instrument with strings.

Clef—A sign written at the beginning of each line of music to give precise pitch meaning to the staff. *32–34*

Close harmony—Harmony in which the chords are arranged with the minimum spread between the highest and lowest tones.

Close position—The spacing of chords with less than an octave between the soprano and tenor parts. *136*

Coda—Tail; the concluding section of a musical form. *148*

Codetta—A small coda.

Color—Timbre or distinctive quality of a tone.

Coloratura—Virtuoso passages in vocal music characterized by rapid runs, turns, trills, and similar devices. Also, a soprano voice that performs coloratura music as a specialty.

Come—As, like.

Commodo—Convenient, comfortable.

Common chord—A chord that occurs in two keys.

Common time—Four-four time. *17*

Common tone—A tone that occurs in two keys or chords.

Compass—The pitch range of a voice, instrument, part, or chord.

Compound interval—An interval larger than an octave. *95*

Compound meter, compound time—A meter in which the number of beats is a multiple of 3. *16, 18*

Con—With.

Concord—An agreeable combination of notes.

Conducting patterns—20

Conjunct—Stepwise.

Consonance—A harmonious combination of tones that does not require resolution.

Continuo—See Basso Continuo.

Contra—Against; as a prefix, denotes a lower octave.

Contralto—A low female voice; same as alto.
Contrapuntal—Pertaining to counterpoint; polyphonic.
Counterpoint—The art of combining melodies with or without imitation.
Crescendo (cresc.)—Increasing in loudness. *147*
Cut time—2/2 or *alla breve*. *17*
Da—By, from, for, of.
Da capo (D.C.)—From the beginning. *148*
Dal segno (D.S.)—From the sign. *149*
Deceptive cadence—The progression V to VI.
Decibel—One-tenth of a bel.
Deciso—With decision, resolution.
Decrescendo (decres., decresc.)—Decreasing in loudness. *147*
Degree—One of the tones of a scale.
Del, della, delle, dello—Of the.
Détaché—Detached. A style of bowing on string instruments in which up- and down-strokes alternate on successive notes.
Diatonic—Natural, not sharp or flat. In or from the scale.
Diminished interval—A half step smaller than perfect or minor. *96, 97, 98*
Diminuendo (dim., dimin.)—Decreasing in loudness. *147*
Diminution—Decreased, usually halved, rhythmic values.
Di molto—Very, extremely.
Discord—A disagreeable combination of notes.
Disjunct—Not stepwise.
Dissonance—A combination of tones that requires resolution.
Divisi (div.)—Divided; directs section in an orchestra or band to divide and play two or more parts.
Dolce (dol.)—Sweet and soft.
Dolcissimo (dolciss.)—Superlative of dolce.
Dolendo, dolente, doloroso—Doleful, plaintive.
Dominant—The fifth degree of a scale or the chord built on it. *120–122*
Doppio—Double. *147*
Dorian—One of the church modes. *85, 86, 87*
Dot—A mark added to a note to increase its rhythmic value by one half. A second dot adds one half the value of the first; a third adds one half the value of the second. *2–3*
Double-augmented—A half step larger than augmented. *97*
Double bar—Two adjacent bar lines that mark the end of a work or major section. *15*
Double-diminished—A half step smaller than diminished. *97*
Double-flat—An accidental that lowers a note a whole step. *39*
Double-sharp—An accidental that raises a note a whole step. *39*
Drink to Me Only with Thine Eyes—*21*
D.S.—Abbreviation for dal segno. *149*
Duodecuple—Twelve-tone. *47, 89*
Duple meter—A meter consisting of two beats, the first of which is accented. *15, 16, 18*
Duplet—Two notes that divide equally the normal duration of three. *7*
Dynamic marks—The words, abbreviations, signs, and symbols used in music to indicate degrees of loudness. *147*
E—And.
Ecclesiastical modes—The church modes. *85–87*
Ed—And.
Embellishment—An ornamental tone or group of tones.
Embouchure—The disposition of the lips and tongue in relation to the mouthpiece of a wind instrument.
Encore—A piece repeated or added in response to applause.
Energico (energ.)—With energy.
Enharmonic tones—Tones with the same pitch written differently. *38–39, 47*
Equal temperament—A system of tuning in which the octave is divided into twelve equal intervals.
Equal voices—Voices of the same type.
Espressivo (espr., espress.)—With expression.

Expression marks—All the directions, excluding only the notation of pitches and rhythms, that guide performers in the interpretation of music.

F clef—The bass clef with F on the fourth line.

Fermata—A hold or pause. *148*

Feroce—Ferocious.

Fervore, con—With fervor.

Figured bass—A bass part with arabic numerals to indicate chords. *122–124*

First inversion—The inversion of a chord with the third in the bass. *110, 111–112*

Fixed do—A system for naming notes in which C is always *do*, D is always *re*, etc. *48 fn.*

Final—In the church modes, the equivalent of the tonic. *86*

Fine—End; marks the concluding point after a return to the beginning or to a sign. *148*

Flag—A part of the symbol for single eighth notes and shorter notes. *3–4, 8*

Flat—A symbol that lowers the pitch of a note a half step. *31, 37–38*

Florid—Ornamented and animated melodic motion.

For He's a Jolly Good Fellow—*21*

Forte (f)—Loud. *147*

Forte-piano (fp)—Loud, then immediately soft. *147*

Fortissimo (ff)—Superlative of forte. *147*

Forza, con—With force.

Forzando (fz)—Forced, strongly accented. *147*

Forzato—Forced, strongly accented.

Fundamental—The root of a chord. The generator of a series of harmonics.

Fuoco, con—With fire.

G clef—The treble clef; G is on the second line of the staff. *31–32, 34*

Gebrauchsmusik—Practical, utilitarian music often intended for performance by amateurs.

Generator—The perceived tone that establishes pitch, as opposed to the overtones or harmonics that account for timbre.

Giocoso—Playful.

Giusto—Just, strict, exact.

Glissando—A sliding pitch effect.

Grace—An ornamenting melodic note or figure.

Grace note—An embellishing note played quickly in time stolen from an adjacent note. Written as a small note symbol, usually with a diagonal line across the stem. *151*

Grandioso—With grandeur, majesty.

Grand pause (G.P.)—Silence. A general rest for the entire orchestra or ensemble. *149*

Grave—Solemn, serious, slow.

Grazioso—Graceful.

Great staff—The combination of a staff with a treble and a staff with a bass clef. *35*

Ground bass—A phrase repeated continuously in the bass.

Gruber—*Silent Night*. *28*

Half cadence—An incomplete cadence, usually on dominant harmony.

Half step—A semitone. The smallest interval. *37*

Hansel and Gretel—Humperdinck. *106*

Harmonic—Pertaining to harmony.

Harmonic minor—The minor scale pattern with a raised seventh degree (leading tone). *72–73*

Harmonics—Overtones.

Harmony—The sounding together of tones. Also, the study of chords and progressions.

Hold—A fermata; a sign indicating a prolongation of rhythmic value. *148*

Homophonic—A type of musical texture in which the melody, usually in the highest part, is supported by chords or an accompaniment.

Homophony—Homophonic music.

Hook—See Flag.

Humperdinck—*Hansel and Gretel*. *106*

Hypo—A prefix denoting a specific range in the church modes. *87*

Imitation—The immediate repetition in another part of a melody or melodic element.

Imitative counterpoint—Counterpoint with imitation.

Impressionism—A musical style of the late nineteenth and early twentieth centuries, with which Debussy and Ravel are particularly associated.

Incalcando, incalzando (incal.)—Pressing forward. *147*

Inharmonic tone—Same as nonchord tone.

Interpretation—The personal and creative contributions of performers beyond the reproduction of pitches and rhythms.

Interval—The difference in pitch between two notes. *95–99*
   Augmented—*96, 97, 98*
   Compound—*95–96*
   Diminished—*96, 97, 98*
   Double augmented—*97*
   Double diminished—*97*
   Harmonic—*95*
   Major—*96, 97, 98*
   Melodic—*95*
   Minor—*96, 97, 98*
   Perfect—*96, 97, 98*

Intonation—The adjustment of pitch to uniform standards.

Inversion—Changing the order from bottom to top of notes of an interval, members of a chord, or lines of a counterpoint. *97, 110, 111–112*

Ionian—The church mode that corresponds with major. *85, 86, 87*

Istesso—Same.

Just intonation—A system of tuning and intonation based on the vibrating frequency ratios 2:3 and 4:5 of the perfect fifth and major third, respectively.

Key—Tonality; the scale and the relationships embodied in it. See *Signature, Key.* Also, the mechanism of an instrument activated by the fingers.

Keyboard—The keys collectively on pianos, organs, etc. *38, 39*

Keynote—The first note of the scale and the central tone of the key. *49, 58–60, 74*

Key signature—See *Signature, Key.*

Lamentoso—Lamentingly, mournfully.

Larghetto—Diminutive of large; slightly less slow than largo. *146*

Larghissimo—Superlative of largo. *146*

Largo—Broad, large, very slow, the slowest tempo indication. *146*

L'Arlésienne—Bizet. *80*

Leading tone—The seventh degree of the scale, a half step below the tonic.

Leap—A melodic interval larger than a second.

Ledger lines—See *Leger Lines.*

Legato (leg.)—Bound, a manner of playing in which successive notes are played smoothly, joined without separation.

Leger lines—Short lines used to represent pitches above and below the staff. *31, 35*

Leggero, leggiero (legg.)—Lightly.

Lento—Slow, but not so slow as largo. *146*

Ligature—See *Beam.*

L'istesso tempo—The same tempo.

Loco—As written; used after an octave sign. *35*

Locrian—One of the church modes. *86, 87*

Lunga—Long.

Lusingando—Seductively.

Lydian—One of the church modes. *86, 87*

Lyric—Songlike rather than epic or dramatic.

Ma—But.

Madrigal—An early secular vocal form for three to eight unaccompanied voices.

Maestoso—Majestically.

Maggiore—Major.

Major—Intervals a half-step larger than minor. *96*
   Scale—The scale pattern produced by the natural notes starting on C. *48–51*

Marcato (marc.)—Marked, stressed.

Marziale—Martial.

Measure—A metric unit consisting of a specific number and pattern of beats delineated by bar lines. *15*
  Incomplete—*22*

Mediant—The third degree of the scale or the chord built on it. *120–122*

Melodic minor—The minor scale pattern with raised sixth and seventh degrees. *73*

Meno—Less.

Meno moso, meno moto—Less movement, slower. *147*

Menuetto—A minuet.

Meter—The number of beats and the pattern of accents in a measure. *15–17, 18*

Metronome—A device used to measure and regulate tempo. *145*

Mezzo—Half.

Mezzo soprano—The female voice lower than soprano but higher than alto.

Mezzo forte (mf)—Half loud; rather loud but not so loud as *forte*. *147*

Mezzo piano (mp)—Half soft; rather soft but not so soft as *piano*. *147*

Microtone—An interval smaller than a semitone.

Middle ages—The period of music roughly from 500 to 1450.

Middle C—The C midway between the treble and the bass clefs. *33–34*

Minor—An interval a half step smaller than major. *96*
  Scale—A scale the characteristic feature of which is a half step between the second and third degrees. *71–73*

Minore—Minor.

Minuet—A graceful dance in moderate triple (¾) meter, and the music inspired by it. Often the third movement in symphonies, sonatas, and similar works.

Misterioso—Mysteriously.

Misura—Measure; exact time.

Mixolydian—One of the church modes. *86, 87*

M.M., Mälzel metronome—An indication of tempo. The number following the abbreviation is the number of beats per minute. *145–146*

Modal—Pertaining to or derived from a church mode; neither major nor minor.

Mode—A scale form. References to the mode of music written before 1600 usually imply one of the church modes. References to the mode of subsequent music generally imply either major or minor. *85–87*

Moderato—Moderate. *146*

Modulation—A change of key during the course of a composition.

Molto—Very.

Monophonic, monophony—Music consisting of a single, unaccompanied melody.

Morendo (mor.)—Dying away, fading.

Mosso, moto—Motion.

Motet—Typically, a polyphonic composition with a sacred, Latin text for unaccompanied voices.

Movable do—The system of syllables in which the keynote is *do*. *48fn.*

Movement—One of the more or less independent sections of a symphony, sonata, suite, or similar work.

Musicology—The scientific study of all branches of music except composition and performance, with emphasis upon history and research.

Mute—A device for softening and modifying the sound of certain instruments.

Natural—A note that is neither sharp nor flat. Also, the sign that cancels sharps and flats. *31, 37, 57*

Natural minor—The form of minor that corresponds with the key signature. *71–72*

Non—Not.

Nonchord tone—A tone not in the prevailing chord.

Nonharmonic tone—Same as nonchord tone.

Notes—The pitch and rhythm symbols in music. The tones they represent are also often referred to as notes. *1–3, 8*

Nuances—Subtle expressive shadings, largely unnotated, in a performance.

Obbligato (obbli.)—Obligatory, necessary.

Octave (8, 8va)—The interval represented by two notes with the same letter name and a vibrating frequency ratio of 1:2. *35–36*

..n position—Chord spacing with an octave or more between the soprano and tenor. *136.*

..pus (op.)—A musical composition (usually associated with a number). Works of a composer are numbered consecutively, ordinarily in order of publication.

Ornaments—More or less unessential notes used to embellish melodic lines.

Ossia—Or else; indicates an alternative version.

Ostinato—Obstinate; a figure or phrase that is repeated continuously during a passage.

Ottave (8, 8va)—Octave.

Overtones—Components of musical tones generated by the fundamental which give each instrument or voice its distinctive quality or timbre.

Parallel major and minor keys—Keys sharing the same keynote. *74–75*

Parlando—As if speaking.

Pause—A hold or fermata. *148*

Pentatonic scale—A five-tone scale usually with the pattern of the black keys of the piano. *87–88*

Perdendosi (Perd.)—Dying away.

Pesante (Pes.)—Heavy.

Phrygian—One of the church modes. *86, 87*

Piacevole—Agreeable.

Pianissimo (pp)—Superlative of *piano*. *147*

Piano (p)—Soft. Also, the common name for the pianoforte. *147*

Pianoforte—The original, proper name for the piano.

Pitch—The aspect of tone determined by vibrating frequency of the fundamental. *31–39*

Piu—More.

Piu mosso, piu moto—More motion, faster. *147*

Pizzicato (Pizz.)—Plucked. A method of producing tones on stringed instruments.

Poco—Little.

Poi—Then.

Polychord—A combination of two or more different chords. *113–114*

Plagal cadence—The harmonic progression IV to I as a cadence.

Polyphonic, polyphony—Music with two or more independent parts forming a contrapuntal texture.

Polytonality—The presence simultaneously of two or more tonal centers or keys.

Pomposo—Pompously.

Portamento—A special manner of approaching the pitch ultimately desired through a glide.

Prestissimo—Superlative of *presto;* the fastest tempo indication. *146*

Presto—Very fast. *146*

Prima volta—The first time.

Prime—Unison. *95*

Program music—Music with literary or pictorial connotations, as opposed to absolute music, which has none.

Pulse—The beat. *15*

Quadruple meter—A meter of four beats in which the first is a primary accent, the third is a secondary accent, and the second and fourth are unaccented. *16, 17, 18*

Quartal harmony—Chords constructed in fourths.

Quasi—As if, in the manner of.

Quintuplet—Five equal notes played in the time value of four. *7*

Rallentando (rall.)—Gradually slowing. *147*

Range—The pitches a voice or instrument can produce from lowest to highest.

Recitative (recit.)—A passage in declamatory style for solo voice with simple accompaniment, or an instrumental passage imitating this effect.

Related keys—Those keys that have most of their notes in common.

Relative minor and major keys—Keys sharing the same key signature. *74–75*

Remote keys—Those keys that have few of their notes in common.

Renaissance—The period of music from about 1450 to 1600.

Repeat signs—An indication that the passage between is to be played twice. *148*

Resolution—The progression of a dissonant interval or chord to a satisfactory consonant interval or chord.

Rest—The notation for silence. *4*

Rhythm—The total temporal aspect of music; the relationships of duration and metrical grouping. *1, 15*

Rinforzando (rf., rfz., rinf.)—Reinforced; suddenly stressed. *147*
Ritardando (rit., ritard.)—Gradually slowing, *147*
Ritenuto—Holding back. Immediately slower. *147*
Romantic—A period of music lasting from about 1825 until near the turn of the present century.
Root—The lowest note of traditional chords when they are arranged in thirds. *110, 111*
Rubato—Robbed; denotes rhythmic freedom with the implication that value taken from one beat or
    measure will be added to another at the discretion of the performer. *147*
Run—A rapidly performed scale.
Scale—A pattern of pitches arranged in ascending or descending order. *47–51, 71–73, 85–89*
   See also *Chromatic, Duodecuple, Church Modes, Major, Minor, Pentatonic, Whole-Tone Scales.*
Scherzando (scherz.)—Playful.
Scherzo—Joke, jest. A brusque, humorous movement or piece in a vivacious triple meter. Sometimes
    used in symphonies, sonatas, etc., in place of a minuet.
Schumann—Choral. *139–140.*
Scintillante—Scintillating.
Sciolto—In a free manner; with license.
Score—A composite of all the parts of a composition.
Scoring—Arranging music for a specific medium.
Secco—Dry.
Second inversion—The inversion of a chord with the fifth in the bass. *110, 111–112*
Secondary chords—Chords built on the second, third, sixth, and seventh degrees of the scale.
Seconda volta—Second time.
Segno—Sign. *149*
Segue—Follows; continue in the same manner.
Semi—Half.
Semitone—Half step. *37*
Semplice—Simply.
Sempre (sem., semp.)—Always; throughout.
Senza—Without.
Senza misura—Unmeasured. *147*
Septuplet—Seven equal notes played in the time value of four or eight. *7*
Sequence—The immediate duplication of a tonal pattern in the same part(s) at a different pitch level.
Serioso—In a serious, somber manner.
Sextuplet—A group of six equal notes played in the time value of four. *7*
Sforzando (sf., sfz.)—Forcing. An explosive accent. *147*
Sforzando piano (sfp.)—Immediately soft after an explosive accent.
Sharp—A symbol that raises the pitch a half step. *31, 37, 38*
Signature, key—The sharps or flats that appear at the beginning of each line of music to indicate the
    tonality. *57*
  Major key—*57–62*
  Minor key—*74–75*
Signature, time or meter—The arabic numerals at the beginning of a work denoting the meter and the
    rhythmic symbol used to represent the beat. *15, 17–20*
Silent Night—Gruber. *28*
Simile (sim.)—Similarly; in the same manner.
Simple intervals—Intervals of an octave or less. *95*
Sin' al—Until the.
Six chord—A first inversion of a triad.
Six-four chord—A second inversion of a triad.
Skip—A melodic interval exceeding a second.
Slargando, slargandosi, slargato, slentando—Slowing. *147*
Slur—A curved line above or below notes of a phrase that are to be joined smoothly; sung or played
    with a single breath or stroke of the bow. *149*
Smorzato (smorz.)—Dying away.
Soave, soavemente—Suave, gentle.
Solenne, solennemente—Solemn.
Sol-fa syllables—A collective name for syllables.
Solfège, solfeggio—Singing with syllables.

Tonic—The keynote. The first note of the scale and the central note of the key. *120–122*
Tonic sol-fa—A *movable do* system of syllables.
Tosto—Swift, rapid.
Tranquillamente, tranquillo—Tranquilly.
Transpose—To write or play at a different pitch level either in a different octave or in a different key.
Treble clef—The G clef, with G on the second line. *32–33, 34*
Tremolo—Trembling; the rapid reiteration of one note or the rapid alternation of two.
Triad—A three-note chord composed of alternate scale tones. *109–110*
    Primary—122
    Secondary—122
    Structure—109–110
    Symbols—119–120
Trill (tr.)—The rapid alternation of a principal note with an auxiliary note a second above. *150*
Trio—Either a group of three performers, a composition written in three parts, or the middle section of a minuet or scherzo, originally written for three instruments.
Triple meter—A meter of three beats with the first accented. *15, 16, 18*
Triplet—Three equal notes played in the time value of two. *7*
Tritone—The augmented fourth. *98*
Troppo—Too much.
Twelve-tone technique—A twentieth century system of composition utilizing a tone row or series. *89*
Un, uno—One, a, an.
Una corda (u.c.)—One string; on the piano, use the soft pedal.
Unison—A *prime;* at the same pitch. *95*
Upbeat—The note or notes preceding the first primary accent, and the conductor's gesture that accompanies them. *22*
Veloce—Swift, rapid.
Vibrato (vib.)—An effect involving slight fluctuations in pitch or intensity.
Vigore, vigoroso—With vigor.
Vivace—Quick, lively. *146*
Vivacissimo—Very quick, lively. *146*
Vivo—With life.
Volante—Flying.
Volta—Time, turn.
Volti subito (V.S.)—Turn the page quickly. *149*
Whole step—A major second. *38*
Whole tone—A major second. *38*
Whole-tone scale—A six-tone scale without half steps. *89*